Where was this book when I was in High School?! Even though I was in church most Sundays, I still had many questions about God and life. Being young doesn't mean that one has unlimited time to seek and search out meaningful answers to the big questions. Besides that, who do you trust and where do you start? Back then, the last thing I wanted to do was spend my free time in the back of the library perusing the dark and dusty 'religion' section. But you don't have to. Included in this book are very important questions and meaningful answers. No judgement, no drama, just good biblical thought. Everyone has time for that. Thanks David.

Angela MacKenzie
Vice President, SuperChannel, Gospel musician, Pianist

We live in a time when so many questions about the Christian faith and current issues feel like they've become weaponised. I love David Robertson's fearless and friendly way of stepping into the path of sticky and sometimes confronting questions that can flummox, threaten and confuse young and old alike. I love how, with carefully chosen words and a smile you feel rise out of the page, David respects the question and the questioner as he shapes his thoughtful, biblical and economical answers in a way that is so substantial and understandable. And I love how a book David has written for youth turns out to be such valuable resource for all of us!

Colin Buchanan
Christian Children's Recording artist and author
Sydney, Australia

SEEK is an awesome book for teenagers. It's filled with great questions and even better answers. The chapters have interesting topics and it helps you see just how amazing God is.

Abby O'Brien
Sydney, Australia (age 13)

This book is remarkable in its scope, depth and simplicity. It takes the issues of our day, exposes them to a biblical worldview and then leaves the reader with questions to ponder, relevant and thought-provoking reading and a model prayer to pray. My twelve-year-old son told me: 'It tells you the truth, even when it's controversial.'

Rico Tice
Author and Founder of Christianity Explored Ministries

This book is a useful tool in tackling questions about current world topics that young Christians and people exploring Christianity have. The book covers a broad range of content from questions about school to more complex things. Personally, I really enjoyed how the book clearly explains what the Bible has to say about these topics and how it always ends in prayer. This book educates you on question you may have or might not have even thought of yet!

Haylee O'Grady
Australian teenager

This book explains confusing issues in life. It's a glimmer of light in a world of darkness.

Peter Tice
(age 12)

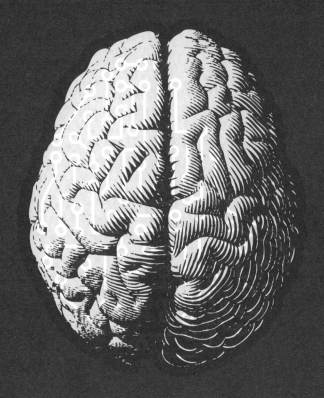

SEEK.

MORE REAL WORLD QUESTIONS / MORE REAL WORD ANSWERS

DAVID ROBERTSON

Scripture quotations are from the *Holy Bible, New International Version*. Copyright © 1973, 1978, 1984 by International Bible Society. Used by permission of Hodder & Stoughton Publishers, A member of the Hodder Headline Group. All rights reserved. "NIV" is a registered trademark of International Bible Society. U.K. trademark number 1448790.

10 9 8 7 6 5 4 3 2 1

Hardback ISBN 978-1-5271-0705-2
ebook ISBN 978-1-5271-1061-8

Published in 2023
by Christian Focus Publications, Ltd.
Geanies House, Fearn,
Ross –shire, IV20 1TW, Scotland.
www.christianfocus.com

Cover and page design by Moose77.com

Printed and bound by
Bell and Bain, Glasgow

INTRODUCTION

Welcome to *SEEK* a second book of questions from teenagers all over the world. In the first, *ASK*, we found that these questions are ones asked by all kinds of people. The title came from the words of Jesus – 'Ask and it will be given to you; seek and you will find; knock and the door will be opened to you. For everyone who asks receives; the one who seeks finds; and to the one who knocks, the door will be opened.' (Matthew 7:7-8). In *SEEK* we have fifty-two new questions, covering issues from society, education, the Bible, theology, God and more. The purpose of these books is not to give you a manual with all the right answers – but to encourage you to think biblically for yourself. These are real world questions – and there are real word answers.

The format is the same as *ASK*. There are fifty-two short chapters. Each contains a question, a Bible passage, a Bible verse, a discussion, something to consider, suggested further reading and a prayer. Please note that just because I suggest a book or books to read, does not mean that I agree with everything in it – nor that you should. Just as you don't have to agree with everything in this book. There is only one book that is infallible!

We are meant to think for ourselves. We can read and learn from those who we don't always agree with! Also be aware that books are varied in depth and quality – some were written for teenagers, some short, some long – but I hope that all of them are helpful. Of course I don't expect you to read them all – but they are there for you to follow up any particular questions.

I love the promise that Jesus gives to those who seek – they shall find! There are people who spend their lives seeking for things that don't matter – and are dissatisfied when they find them. There are others who spend their lives seeking for things that don't exist – like the lost city of Atlantis or the Loch Ness monster (I realise that is a little controversial!). But when Jesus talks about seeking, he is talking about us looking for the God who really matters, the God who really exists. In some way, all of our questions lead to him.

Perhaps the most common thing that people say they are seeking is happiness. But what is happiness? How do we get it? How do we keep it? As we go through the questions that young people sent to me, some may appear to be relatively trivial, others really important – but all of them ultimately find their answer in Christ. And that is true about the question of happiness. Jesus says he came to give us life – real life, eternal life, joyous life.

Perhaps it will help us to think of seeking like this:

Search – what is happening? How do we find meaning, purpose, understanding, love and happiness?

Educate – In a world of lies, fake news and fear, how can we know? Education can just simply mean getting instruction – which is what happens at school. But it can also mean 'an enlightening experience'. I hope that as you read through SEEK and think about things for yourself that you will be educated and enlightened.

Engage – We are not really interested in just learning about things. We really want to know them. Imagine if you could learn all about ice cream – how it was made, what it consists of etc. and yet you never tasted it! I would love *SEEK* to encourage you to taste and see that God is good.

Knock – I'm going to leave it to the end to tell you what this part is …

There is an old band called The Who who have a great song called *The Seeker*. In it they state:

> They call me The Seeker
> I've been searching low and high
> I won't get to get what I'm after
> Till the day I die

When you are younger you tend to ask a lot of questions. That is a good thing. Sometimes as people get older, they become more cynical and doubt that there are any real answers. I don't have all the answers – and some of the questions are complex – but I do know the One who does. Each of the answers in this book is meant to help you in your search and encourage you to think for yourself and find out answers. You don't have to wait until the day you die to get answers. As Jesus said, 'seek and you will find.'

David Robertson

PS. There are some questions in *SEEK* which are linked to questions in *ASK*. To avoid repetition where this is the case I mention that in the answer.

CONTENTS

1. CLIMATE CHANGE

QUESTION: Do you think climate change is real? Will the World be destroyed from climate change?

BIBLE READING: Romans 8:18-22

TEXT: '... in hope that the creation itself will be liberated from its bondage to decay and brought into the freedom and glory of the children of God' (Romans 8:21).

When I was a teenager, I remember reading in the *Readers Digest Atlas of the World* a depressing statement that the whole universe would, in a few billion years, either implode or explode into destruction. Even then it seemed to me a pretty hopeless view of the future. Bertrand Russell once wrote 'all the labours of the ages, all the devotion, all the inspiration, all the noonday brightness of human genius, are destined to extinction in the vast death of the solar system, and that the whole temple of Man's achievement must inevitably be buried beneath the debris of a universe in ruins' (*A Free Man's Worship*). Again, pretty hopeless.

I thought of that when I came across a group of teenagers in Sydney city centre campaigning against climate change. When I began discussing with them – they got both angry and afraid. 'Don't you care? The world is going to end in twelve years!' It was a somewhat apocalyptic view – and yet I could see one that they genuinely believed in. A couple of decades ago the people you saw on the street corners with the sign 'the end is nigh' were often Christians of an apocalyptic persuasion – now it's Green activists. Do they have a point? What does the Bible have to say on this issue?

I love Romans 8. Indeed, it is a chapter of the Bible that I most often reflect on. Not least because in the passage referred to, we are given real hope for the creation. Yes, I do believe that there is such a thing as climate change and that what humanity does has an effect upon the climate. It is a matter of considerable debate just how much effect, and what is the best way to deal with that. But, as regards your question – no, the world will not be destroyed from climate change. In *ASK* we looked at the question of the end of the world (*ASK* 23) and saw that it is God who will bring about the end of the world, not humanity. He does so not in order to destroy all things but to renew them.

Now in this passage we are told that the whole creation is waiting. Waiting for what? The creation is frustrated. It is in bondage to decay. It groans as in the pains of childbirth. That is what the earthquakes, diseases and extreme weather events are. And the creation is waiting for these to be removed and its rebirth to take place. That will only happen when the children of God will be revealed. That is an amazing truth. It means that the best thing you and I can do for the creation, is to communicate the Good News of Jesus Christ, so that more people will believe and become the children of God. It is good for us to take care of the environment – to avoid as much pollution as we can and to be good stewards of what God has placed us in charge of. After all, he does warn us that on the day of judgement, he will destroy those who destroy the earth (Revelation 11:18). But the best way for us to take care of the creation is to proclaim the Creator.

Gus Speth was a climate scientist founder and a former chairman of the Council on Environmental Quality. He gave this remarkable testimony: 'I used to think that the top environmental problems were biodiversity loss, ecosystem collapse, and climate change. I thought that thirty years of good science could address these problems. I was wrong. The top environmental problems are selfishness, greed, and apathy, and to deal with these we need a cultural and spiritual transformation. And we scientists don't know how to do that.' But God does.

CONSIDER: Are you concerned about the environment and climate change? What do you think you can do? How can you help your friends who do not have the assurance that God has got the whole world in his hands? What is the bigger picture?

RECOMMENDED FURTHER READING:
A Different Shade of Green – Gordon Wilson
Apocalypse Never: Why Environmental Alarmism Hurts Us All – Michael Shellenberger (This is not a Christian book but it is full of stimulating information and practical ideas)

PRAYER: O Lord, we bless and praise your name that the earth is yours, and everything in it; the world, and all who live on it. (Psalm 24:1). We thank you that it is in your hands not ours. We ask O God, that you would enable us to be good stewards of your creation and that we would seek to communicate the Gospel all over the world so that your children will be revealed, and the creation ultimately set free, in Jesus Name, Amen.

QUESTION: What is a woman? (And man).

BIBLE READING: Proverbs 31:10-31

TEXT: 'Charm is deceptive, and beauty is fleeting; but a woman who fears the Lord is to be praised' (Proverbs 31:30).

The wannabe Supreme Court judge in the U.S., Judge Jackson, was asked a question; which, in any other time before 2020, would have been considered a silly question: 'Can you provide the definition of a woman?' 'No,' she replied, 'I can't, not in this context, I'm not a biologist.' Australia's Secretary of the Department of Health, Dr Brendan Murphy, was asked the same question, by a Senator. Professor Murphy was unable to answer and said that he would 'take it on notice' because it was a 'very contested space'. The Scottish First Minister, Nicola Sturgeon, when asked the same question, refused to answer, claiming that it would 'oversimplify' the debate over gender reform – yet at the same time she claimed to be defending women's rights!

I'm not a biologist. I'm not a professor of health. And I'm not a senior politician. But I can tell you what a woman is. A woman is an adult, human female. It really is that simple. So why all the fuss?

I won't repeat what I said on this subject in *ASK* questions 11 and 36 – but let me add some observations here.

The question itself is deeply misogynistic. By that I mean that when women have to continually defend what a woman is, they are under profound attack. Have you ever noticed that the question is never asked 'what is a man?'. Women who believe that their biological sex is crucial to their being a woman are sometimes called 'TERFs' – that is Trans Exclusionary Radical Feminists. I have yet to hear a man who also wants to defend their biological sex being called a TERM – Trans Exclusionary Radical Male! It is ironic that an idea that came out of people such as the feminist writer, Judith Butler, has now become something which is far more damaging to women's rights than anything a man could come up with! Butler helped develop the whole idea of Queer theory which argued that gender was just a social construct (i.e., something that humans made up in society, and could be changed by society) and that it had nothing to do with biological sex.

The question (and answers) is also deeply confusing. In a school in Scotland a teacher was telling the primary school pupils about the birth of Jesus. 'Mary was a pregnant woman ...' 'No!', shouted one of the girls. 'You can't say that – she could have been a man!' When children are taught that men can become pregnant, that they can be any gender that they want to be, and that there are over 100 plus genders – it is little wonder that they get confused. When judges, doctors and politicians can't tell us what a woman is, how are you as a teenage girl supposed to know?!

The Bible really helps us here. It tells us that all human beings are made in the image of God – and that we are made male and female. If you are a female teenager, you are equal to any male! Both men and women need to remember that.

When God brought the world into being, we are told that he saw that it was good. It is only after everything else, that he pronounced it 'very good'. Human beings are the apex of God's creation – the apple of his eye. That is why the devil seeks to destroy and harm humanity. I can hardly think of anything more harmful than the attempt to de-construct human beings as male and female and turn us into a thousand meaningless genders.

The Bible gives us a clear answer to what a woman is. That gives us the basis for meaning, life and equality. If you are a girl or woman, you must never let that be taken from you. Likewise, if you are a boy or man. It means something. It is not just a social construct – something humanity made up. It is of the very essence of being human.

None of this is to demean or to stigmatise those who struggle with GID – gender identity disorder. But the answer to that disorder is not to seek to reorder the whole world – but rather to seek wholeness and healing in Christ.

CONSIDER: Are you ever confused about what it means to be your gender? What are the basic, foundational differences between male and female? What are only cultural? Do you see why it is important to have a clear understanding of how God made us?

RECOMMENDED FURTHER READING:

What does the Bible Teach about Transgenderism? Owen Strachan and Gavin Peacock.

Irreversible Damage – Abigail Shirer (This book is not a Christian book but is especially helpful for teenage girls and shows how transgender ideology causes so much harm especially to you).

PRAYER: Our Father in heaven, we know that the devil is the father of lies, confusion and deceit. We know that he wants to destroy your works and especially those made in your image. Please protect us and all your people. We pray for those who struggle with gender identity disorder. Help us to love them and to enable them to see that their identity is to be found in you. We pray for women, men and children who have been confused and abused by this wicked, confusing and destructive ideology. Restore humanity to your image in all its glory, in Jesus' name, Amen.

3. CAPITALIST OR COMMUNIST?

QUESTION: Are we progressing to a better world? Is the future Western Capitalism, Chinese communism, or something else?

BIBLE READING: Isaiah 11:1-9

TEXT: 'They will neither harm nor destroy on all my holy mountain, for the earth will be filled with the knowledge of the LORD as the waters cover the sea' (Isaiah 11:9).

What is the future going to be like? What will happen? In chapter 1 we saw that there are some who think the future of the world is going to be very short. The end of the world is nigh! In chapter 2 we saw that some think the future of the world will be that of a remade humanity – where we will be split into hundreds of genders and be able to move freely between them. Both of these are what we call dystopian. The dictionary definition of 'dystopian' is 'an imagined world or society in which people lead wretched, dehumanized, fearful lives'. Filmmakers and authors love this. Just think of *The Truman Show, Planet of the Apes, The Matrix* or *Blade Runner*. Or TV series like *Black Mirror, The Hunger Games* or *The Handmaid's Tale*. Or books like *1984* and *Brave New World*. By the way I am not recommending any of these – they are illustrative of a particular genre – one that is getting more and more popular.

People have always anticipated or feared the end of the world. But what is strange is that alongside the increase in dystopian books and movies, most of us are brought up to believe in the inevitability of human progress. When Tony Blair was elected as the Prime Minister of Great Britain on May 1st, 1997, his theme song was D:Ream's 'Things Can Only Get Better'. Many people believe that. The human race is evolving. We are 'progressing' from out of the slime, we are moving on from the ancients, we are leaving the Dark Ages and striding forward to an enlightened brave new world. That is why they speak of the 'wrong side of history'. If you don't accept their values and views, then they think you are backward and on the wrong side of history – they of course are on the right!

But belief in the inevitable progress of humanity is not only delusional, but also dangerous. Why? The belief is delusional because it is not true. Of course, there have been improvements in science, communication and technology. This has brought many advantages for us. But they don't necessarily make all human life better. We can now fight wars more mechanically, spread lies more easily and destroy creation more quickly. Are we really more intelligent than the ancient Greeks? Are we more musical than Beethoven? Are we better writers than Shakespeare and Dante? Better philosophers than Confucius and Pascal? Are we better people than our ancestors?

The dangerous part comes when people believe that if only their system was in power (communism, capitalism or any of the other 'isms') then things would just get better. And if it doesn't, they blame the 'other' – with dreadful consequences. Hitler believed in inevitable progress and thought it would be achieved if the Jews, Slavs, disabled and other groups could just be got out of the way!

Today in the Western world we have 'progressive' elites who think that if only we all follow their self – evidently good values, then we will live in Utopia. When that doesn't happen – they too look for someone to blame. I suspect that Bible-believing Christians are high up on the list!

The trouble is that those who label themselves progressives are in reality 'regressives'. As they reject Christianity, they are going backwards to the values and practices of the pre-Christian Greco/Roman/Pagan world, not advancing into a new era of human progress.

Does that mean that we should despair? Is the world going to inevitably decline? Should Christians basically get in the lifeboats? No – we have a far greater hope. As our passage Isaiah 11 – amongst many others – states. Isaiah looks forward to a time when the earth will be filled with the knowledge of the Lord as the waters cover the sea. That is a time when death, destruction and decay will be destroyed.

It sounds impossible and it is impossible – for human beings. But not for God. That is whilst we respect politicians, we don't expect or trust them to deliver paradise on earth.

It's good for young people (and others) to take an interest in politics, but please don't let political ideology take the place of Christ. He is the wisdom that this world needs. He is its future. Trust him. And do not fear. He's got the whole world in his hands!

CONSIDER: Why do you think people believe that the world is inevitably getting better? What political ideologies have you been tempted to follow? What can we do to make the world a better place? Why is it good to look for the return of Jesus Christ?

RECOMMENDED FURTHER READING:
That Hideous Strength – C.S. Lewis (This is the third part of Lewis' sci-fi trilogy – and though it was written decades ago it was prophetic in seeing how the Western world would develop). Black Mass – John Gray (This is not a Christian book, but it does show how having utopian beliefs is dangerous. Gray is very good on the analysis but poor on the solution because he does not have Christ. Being Christless means being hopeless!)

PRAYER: Lord Jesus, we thank you that you have promised to bring justice for the poor of the earth. That there will come a time when the whole earth will be filled with your glory. We long for that day of peace and harmony. A day when wars will be no more. We pray that we would be those who long for your coming. Even so, come soon, Lord Jesus. Amen.

QUESTION: Why does God permit disease?

BIBLE READING: Isaiah 53:1-6

TEXT: 'But he was pierced for our transgressions, he was crushed for our iniquities; the punishment that brought us peace was on him, and by his wounds we are healed' (Isaiah 53:5).

Some of us have lived through a unique period of history – for 100 years most of the Western world lived without plague or serious community disease. Of course, there was serious illness, including cancer, dementia and many other fatal and serious illnesses. But some even thought that we had defeated disease. And then along came Covid 19! And the whole world realised just how vulnerable we all are. One tiny virus almost brought the world to a standstill.

We ask why? And there are lots of answers. The most obvious one is human error, but that still doesn't answer the question as to why God permitted it. Some Church leaders were quick to say that this has nothing to do with God. Others say that he caused it, and that it is a punishment for the world's sin. I don't accept either position. We are not in a position to pronounce that God is sending this as a particular punishment – he has not revealed that (unlike for example when he sent the plague as a punishment upon David and the Israelites in 2 Samuel 24). Likewise, I don't believe that anything is outwith the sovereignty and power of God. Which means that Covid did not take him by surprise, nor that he was powerless. The question then becomes, as you correctly put it – why does God permit disease?

We looked at this in the wider sense of all suffering in *ASK* 14. Have a read of that. But perhaps it is easier to explain this from a real -life example. Many years ago, I visited a man who was really angry with God – a God that he said he did not believe in. The conversation went something like this:

'Why are you angry with God?'
'Because he killed my wife'
'What?! Who told you that?'
'Some Christians said that it was God's will that she should die.'
'Well, that was a pretty callous thing for them to say.... God did not kill your wife. What did she die of?'
'Cancer.'
'I'm so sorry to hear that. But the question is really, "Why is there cancer in the world?" And even more important than the why question – is, the what question. "What has God done about it?"'

Anyway, to cut a long story short, he invited me into his house and he and I continued the discussion. Every week for about six weeks I returned to meet with him, as we looked at what the Bible said about how God deals with evil, illness and suffering. Until one day I turned up at the door –

'Please go away.'
'Why? I thought we were getting on well?'
'We are. That's the problem. You're beginning to make sense. And I don't want it to make sense. I prefer to be left in my bitterness and anger.'

It was such a sad moment. Because Isaiah 53 introduces us to God's answer to suffering and disease – the suffering servant, Jesus Christ. He was a man of suffering and familiar with pain. This is not to say that Jesus automatically comes along and cures you of every illness you have instantly. Nor is it to justify those who foolishly said, 'I won't get Covid, because Jesus is my vaccine'. In this sin-sick and disease-ridden world, Jesus is not a vaccine, but he is the ultimate cure. In Revelation 7 there is this beautiful picture of heaven – a place where there is no hunger, thirst, or suffering. A place where God wipes away every tear from our eyes.

Psalm 91 assures us that God will save is 'from the deadly pestilence'. The point is not that being a Christian means you never get sick – the point is that God will save you out of that sickness and that you are on your way to the new heavens and the new earth – where there is no more sickness and death. The cure for disease and death, is the eternal life offered by Christ.

CONSIDER: If a doctor offered you a medicine that would cure your illness and take away your pain – would you take it?

Christ offers eternal life – have you accepted his offer? Do you trust that even in sickness, he will lead you through the valley of the shadow of death and bring you into his house forever? (Psalm 23).

RECOMMENDED FURTHER READING:

Where is God in a Coronavirus World? – John Lennox

PRAYER: Lord God, we know that sin is the sickness. We bless you that you have provided the cure. Jesus Christ, our beautiful Saviour, who experienced death, disease, and condemnation – that we might be set free from them all. We praise you for our suffering Saviour and long for the day when we will be with him in a place where disease and death are no more, in His name, Amen.

5. FACTORY FARMING

BIBLE READING: Exodus 20:1-17

TEXT: '... but the seventh day is a sabbath to the Lord your God. On it you shall not do any work, neither you, nor your son or daughter, nor your male or female servant, nor your animals, nor any foreigner residing in your towns' (Exodus 20:10).

Have you seen the film *Amazing Grace*? If not, I would highly recommend you hunt it down. It is one of my favourite films ever. It portrays the life of William Wilberforce who, as everyone knows, helped end slavery in the British Empire. What many people do not know is that he was also a founding member of the RSPCA (the Royal Society for the Prevention of Cruelty to Animals) on 16th June, 1824. For Wilberforce it was an important part of his Christianity that he cared for animals – and it should be for ours. In *ASK* 20 we considered about whether animals go to heaven, now we ask how we should treat them on earth!

There are some who think this subject is not important. I think it is essential. For two reasons - firstly animals are an essential part of our lives - not least because of the food they provide to keep us alive. And secondly because God says so. Here are just a few of the many Bible passages that address the issue.

Proverbs 12:10: 'The righteous care for the needs of their animals, but the kindest acts of the wicked are cruel.'

Deuteronomy 25:4: 'Do not muzzle an ox while it is treading out the grain.'

Matthew 6:26: 'Look at the birds of the air; they do not sow or reap or store away in barns, and yet your heavenly Father feeds them.'

Psalm 104:14: 'He makes grass grow for the cattle, and plants for people to cultivate— bringing forth food from the earth:

I grew up on a farm. My father looked after pigs and my mother chickens! So, I was delighted to discover Joel Salatin's book *The Marvellous Pigness of Pigs*, a book written about this very subject for Christians. Joel observes 'Jesus clearly said it was okay to relieve a distressed animal on the Sabbath, even though the Sabbath was a day of rest. Indeed, Adam's directive to name the animals shows that God was not interested in just a bunch of "its". God feeds the ravens—an especially nasty bird—and knows even when a sparrow falls.'

As regards the question of factory farming Joel gives a graphic description of industrial 'battery' chicken farming. Here is part of that description. 'Prior to industrialization, the average backyard hen weighed about six pounds and laid

150 to 170 eggs per year. Today's commercial bird weighs as little as three pounds and lays 300 eggs in a year. Unlike her old-fashioned cousin, however, this newfangled industrial bird has some real needs. First, she's extremely fragile. She can't handle rainstorms or frosty nights. Second, she requires exceptionally sophisticated nutrients. If she exercised or ran around, she wouldn't be able to put all her energy into simply laying eggs. Therefore, her activity must be restricted in tiny cages inside CAFOs. To ensure maximum production in as short a time as possible, these buildings use lights in a tightly regulated regimen to simulate ever-increasing day length.'

My mother kept a few chickens at her home in the Highland village of Portmahomack. She took worn out 'industrial' chickens, set them free and fed them on scraps. Within weeks they were producing delicious eggs. The difference between them and the supermarket ones – yes even the so called 'free range' ones – was so astonishing that people travelled from all over to get them. Their shells were stronger, their yolks a deeper yellow, and the taste was so much better. 'Granny Chickens' is loved by all her grandchildren – not least because of her care for her animals. As was 'Grandpa Lambs'!

I love my vegetarian friends, and if you are a vegetarian may the Lord richly bless you in your choice, but the Bible does not insist that we have to be vegetarian. It is not wrong to eat meat. However, how that meat is produced, and how we treat the animals who give us wool, milk, leather and eggs, does matter. It is wrong to mistreat animals. I cannot see any way in which factory farming of animals is anything but sin – and sin does make God angry. So, the answer to your question is yes.

CONSIDER: Do you think about where your food comes from? Would you be prepared to pay a little more money if the animals were treated better? Maybe it's time to think more about how we produce food, how we buy it and how we cook it!

RECOMMENDED FURTHER READING:
The Marvellous Pigness of Pigs: Respecting and Caring for All God's Creation – Joel Salatin

PRAYER: Father God, you give us all things richly to enjoy. Not exploit. Forgive us when we misuse and abuse your gifts. Thank you for your care for the sparrow and for your feeding the lions. Enable us to appreciate the variety in your creation and to be good stewards of it. May we be like our Father in heaven. For your glory. Amen.

6. BLACK LIVES MATTER

QUESTION: Do Black Lives Matter? Was Jesus White? Why should Africans worship a white God?

BIBLE READING: Revelation 7:9-17

TEXT: 'After this I looked, and there before me was a great multitude that no one could count, from every nation, tribe, people and language, standing before the throne and before the Lamb' (Revelation 7:9).

In one way this is a very easy question to answer. Yes, black lives matter. No, Jesus was not white. And no, Africans should not worship a white God. But let's unpack this a little. Starting with the third question.

God is not a white God. God is a Spirit. We human beings create gods in our own image, but the God who created us all, is a pure Spirit. He is not confined to a human body. He does not have a body or a colour of skin – because he does not have skin!

Have you heard of the Shorter Catechism? It is a great summary of Christian doctrine in question and answer form. It can help us here.

Question four asks: 'What is God?'

'God is a Spirit, infinite, eternal, and unchangeable, in his being, wisdom, power, holiness, justice, goodness, and truth.'

But what does the Bible mean when it says that we are made in the image of God (Genesis 1:27)? I like the answer of the Shorter Catechism in question ten: 'How did God create man?' 'God created man male and female, after his own image, in knowledge, righteousness, and holiness, with dominion over the creatures.'

This means everyone. A young African woman spoke to me in Western Sydney and asked about whether she experienced racism because God had made Africans inferior. I spoke to her and gave her *ASK* (question 30), which deals with this wrong belief. All human beings are equally made in the image of God. I was deeply moved by her joyful emotional reaction to what was a biblical truth that I had wrongly assumed everyone knew!

You also need to remember that there are not many gods – where each race or tribe have their own. Again, the Shorter Catechism question 5. 'Are there more Gods than one?' 'There is but one only, the living and true God.'

That is why, in the passage we read about John's vision of heaven, it states that there are many tribes, languages and nations before the throne of God. But there is only one God.

Now, on to Jesus. He, as the Son of God, came to earth as a human being in a particular context. He was born in Israel/Palestine. We don't know what he looked like, because there is no description of him, no photos, no videos and no paintings by eyewitnesses. But we do know that he would have looked like the people around him - who were not white.

What about BLM? Of course, black lives matter, because all human beings, whatever their skin colour are made in the image of God. But because we say that black lives matter that does not mean that we have to support the political organisation which is known as BLM. In fact, there are many things about the BLM movement that should make a Christian hesitant about supporting it. It is hardly an advocate of Christian teaching on God, humanity and the family. For example, as an organisation it supports abortion - don't the lives of black babies matter? Margaret Sanger, the founder of Planned Parenthood, the main abortion provider in the US, was a eugenicist who thought that abortion was a great way to reduce the poor black population!

BLM operate with a philosophy called Critical Race Theory. I don't have time to go into the details of it all but let me say that it is a very dangerous and anti-Christian teaching - stating that white people are racist because of the colour of their skin. Ironically CRT is itself deeply racist - judging people by the colour of their skin. Martin Luther King in his famous 'I have a Dream' speech (look it up!) stated the opposite: 'I have a dream that my four little children will one day live in a nation where they will not be judged by the colour of their skin but by the content of their character.'

As Christians we should recognise that racism and discrimination in the United States has been a particular problem, because of the history of slavery. And we should never underplay the racism that still exists in some sections of society. However, as Christians we also recognise that the United States is not the whole world. We do believe that black lives matter - including the thousands of black Christians who are killed in Nigeria every year, and who never get a mention from the BLM supporters.

We also recognise that racism has existed in every human society since the Fall of humanity. It is not just white people in America or Europe who can be racist . All human beings of any colour of skin can be racist, because all of us are human. The only solution to that is found in Christ. There are no racial or gender divisions between Christians because we are all one in Christ (Galatians 3:28). We are united around the throne worshipping the one true God!

CONSIDER: Are you conscious of any racist attitudes you may have? Are you aware of friends or neighbours who are wrongly treated because of their race? What do you think you can do to help?

RECOMMENDED FURTHER READING:
Faultlines – Voddie Baucham
The Illustrated Westminster Shorter Catechism – Christian Focus Publications

PRAYER: Lord, forgive us when we treat other human beings as though they were not made in your image. Bring unity to your people. We thank you Lord Jesus, that you died for the whole world – red and yellow, black and white – all are precious in your sight. Help us to see that for ourselves and for others. For your glory and our good. Amen.

7. BEING PATRIOTIC

QUESTION: How did you become Scottish? How do you say hallo in Scottish? Can you say, 'they may take our lives, but they will never take our freedom?' Why was I born as a Peruvian and not in another better country like America?

BIBLE READING: Acts 17:16–34

TEXT: 'From one man he made all the nations, that they should inhabit the whole earth; and he marked out their appointed times in history and the boundaries of their lands' (Acts 17:26).

I now live in Sydney, Australia, but like half the population of Australia, I am not an Australian because I was not born here. Sometimes people do ask me your question. They want to hear my Scottish accent – and they want to hear me sound like Mel Gibson, an Australian playing a Scot, in Braveheart! I could become an Australian citizen, but would that make me an Australian? Is nationality to do with where you live? Where were you born? What you feel?

I'm very proud to be Scottish. I love my native land. Although to tell you a wee secret, I was actually born in Berwick-Upon-Tweed, which is technically across the border in England. I suppose I could have decided that I was English - but then I would have had to support the English football team! We don't get to choose our nationality because of the countries we like - they are the countries we are born into - or at least the people we were born into. For example, the English pop singer Cliff Richard was born in India, but he is still very much English.

So, our nationality is tied in with our birth, our parents, where we live and the culture(s) that has shaped us. You are Peruvian, but I am not. But I can tell you that it is a mistake to think that America is a better country than Peru. I have Peruvian friends - and know people who have lived and worked in Peru who think that it is a wonderful country. My church, the Free Church of Scotland, even started a mission work in Peru including a school, Collegio San Andreas (St Andrews school), which is still going strong. You have Machu Picchu and Cusco. Lima and the floating islands of Lake Titicaca. Llamas and alpacas. The Andes and the Amazon. And you have wonderful food, aji amarillo, quinoa, chifa and Peruvian roast chicken. You have music, art, textiles, and literature. And there are lots of Peruvian Christians.

It is always a mistake to think that everywhere else in the world is better than where we are. The grass is always greener on the other side of the fence. When I came to Australia some thought I came because to many British people it sounds like paradise - it is a rich country, with lots of beaches and even more sunshine. But since we have been here there has been drought, bushfires, plague and now floods! The point is that every country has good points and bad points.

It's not just that every country is part of God's good creation, or that it is inhabited by those who are made in the image of God – even though we are fallen sinners. It is also, as Paul told the Athenians, that God has made all the nations and set the boundaries of their lands. We all have our times, places and seasons. This does not mean that God set up Peru, America, Scotland or Australia. To claim that would be wrong. Sometimes I hear people speak of their country as though it were the promised land – that is a sinful nationalistic pride which at best is delusional, at worst dangerous. But it does mean that you and I should not waste time wishing we were in another place or at another time. We have to recognise that God is sovereign, and we should be thankful for where we are and what we have been called to do.

This does not mean that we can never move to another country, or see our circumstances change – but it does mean that we should be asking – not 'why did you not make me an American, (or if you have a greater ambition – Scottish!) – but rather – what can I do to live for your glory in the place and time you have called me to?

Most of all we want to see Christ glorified throughout the whole world, including our countries. In *ASK* 31 we looked at North Korea and the difficulties in living there. We should pray and hope for every country in the world.

CONSIDER: What do you like about your country – or where you now live? What are the bad things? Can you do anything to improve them? How can you best serve God in your country?

RECOMMENDED FURTHER READING:

The Land of the Book - Scottish Christianity in a Year of Quotes - Christian Heritage

John Knox - The Sharpened Sword - Catherine Mackenzie.

At the Roots of a Nation: The Story of Colegio San Andrés, a Christian School in Lima, Peru - John Macpherson

PRAYER: Sovereign Lord, we praise your name that you have marked out our appointed times and set the boundaries of the nations. We thank you for the great variety of cultures and countries. Grant that, wherever we live, we may seek you, love you and serve you - to the glory of your name and the good of all the peoples. For you are the King of Kings. Amen.

8. ABORTION

QUESTION: As abortion is regarded as a sin and the murder of the unborn by people such as yourself, why do evangelical preachers like you not push for widespread effective contraception to be made freely available? Is abortion a sin if the mother would die because of the pregnancy?

BIBLE READING: Psalm 139

TEXT: 'I praise you because I am fearfully and wonderfully made; your works are wonderful,
I know that full well.
My frame was not hidden from you
when I was made in the secret place,
when I was woven together in the depths of the earth.
Your eyes saw my unformed body;
all the days ordained for me were written in your book
before one of them came to be' (Psalm 139:14-16).

We need to unpack this question a little, before answering it. By 'people such as myself' I assume you mean Christians? i.e., those who follow the teachings of Jesus as given to us in his Word. In that regard your question ends up with three parts.

Firstly, is abortion sin? Is it wrong in the eyes of God? Abortion is the unnecessary taking of a human life. Therefore, it is clearly a terrible sin. (Bear in mind that abortion is not the unforgivable sin – there is mercy at the cross of Christ for all sins). But what about all the arguments that are used to defend abortion? It's the mother's body. That might be a valid argument if there was only one body involved. But there are at least two others – the father (it takes two to make a baby) and most importantly that of the baby. There is no doubt that scientifically and biblically (see the above passage) the baby in the womb is a human baby. We should no more give any one the right to take the life of their child in the womb, than we would give it to them when the child is out of the womb. That is the most basic position.

But what about when the mother's life is in danger? In theory it could be argued that if it was a clear choice between the life of the mother and the life of the baby – a choice has to be made. But how often does that choice have to be made? In 2011 a UK government minister told the House of Lords that 'Between 1968 and 2011 (the latest year for which figures are available) there have been 6.4 million abortions performed on residents of England and Wales. Of these, 143 (0.006 per cent) were performed under Section 1(4), i.e., where the termination is immediately necessary to save the life of the pregnant woman or to prevent grave permanent injury to the physical or mental health of the pregnant woman.'

There are those who have argued that the 'saving the mother's life' argument is hypothetical and that 'there are no circumstances in which the life of the mother may only be saved by directly terminating the life of her child' (letter to the Irish Times in 1992 from five of Ireland's top gynaecologists). Dr C Everett Koop, the former Surgeon General of the US declared: 'In my thirty-six years in paediatric surgery I have never known of one instance where the child had to be aborted to save the mother's life.'

Another argument that is often used is that of the dangers of illegal abortions. It is asserted that if abortion is not legal then millions of women will die because of badly carried out abortions. But is this true? Dr Calum Miller of the University of Oxford has done a great deal of work in this area, largely debunking this myth. Read this article in Christian Today – https://www.christiantoday.com/article/abortion.myths.and. realities.a.case.study.from.africa/137772.htm

What about contraception? Should 'people like me' be arguing for widespread effective contraception to be made free? Again, it all depends on what you mean. One of the most effective ways of avoiding unwanted pregnancies is to avoid sexual relations altogether. Christians argue that sex is so special it should be confined to marriage. But what about situations within a marriage where a couple do not want any more children?

There are different Christian views. The Roman Catholic Church for example is totally opposed to contraception. Some evangelicals share that view – arguing that children are a blessing from the Lord, and we should not view them as otherwise. But some hold to the view of conditional permission

– that is that contraception is permitted if it does not destroy human life and is not done for selfish reasons.

The Christian approach to all of this is vastly different from that of much of contemporary society. We value all life as sacred. That is our foundational premise. Which means that we do not have the right to take life at any stage. It is desperately sad and wicked that what should be the safest place in the world for a baby (the womb) has become one of the most dangerous.

CONSIDER: Why do you think people want abortions? What can be done to help those who are scared of bringing a child into the world? How can we offer support and help to those who have had abortions and now come to regret it?

RECOMMENDED FURTHER READING:

There are so many resources I can only point to a few. For more information on this subject look at the websites of organisations like the Society for the Protection of the Unborn Child (SPUC); Evangelicals for Life; Right to Life etc. Two books I would recommend are:

Right to Choose – The Effects of Post Abortion Trauma – Maureen Long
Counter Culture – David Platt

PRAYER: O Lord, we read that in the days of Noah you were deeply troubled that you had made human beings on the earth – because 'every inclination of the thoughts of the human heart was only evil all the time' (Genesis 6:5). What must you think of today? When we justify evil of killing the unborn as a 'human right'! Lord, have mercy on us. Forgive us our sins. Heal those who have been wounded by the deceit of abortion. And grant that we may defend the unborn, and look after the born, in Jesus' name. Amen.

8. OBEYING THE GOVERNMENT

BIBLE READING: Romans 13:1-7

TEXT: 'Let everyone be subject to the governing authorities, for there is no authority except that which God has established. The authorities that exist have been established by God' (Romans 13:1).

All of us as human beings have relationships with other human beings. We are in families, friendships, communities, churches and we are all part of civic societies which are governed by governments. In today's world there is a great deal of cynicism about politicians, and many of us have concerns about governmental overreach, but it still remains the case that we have a responsibility to obey the laws of the land. We are, in the words of our text, to be 'subject to the governing authorities'.

The State is the government of human society, to enable that society to function. Its duty is to ensure that all its members are protected and provided for; to maintain order and peace and to do so by enforcing the rule of law. Peter tells us that we are to submit ourselves 'for the Lord's sake to every authority instituted amongst men' (1 Peter 2:13).

Is that obedience absolute? Should we ever disobey? Yes – because the State has limits. It is not all powerful. However, those limits are decided by God – not by us. We don't get to pick and choose which laws we should obey. But when the law of the State comes into conflict with the law of God – then Christians have an obligation to obey God rather than men.

In sixteenth-century Scotland a Presbyterian minister, Andrew Melville, was called before King James, to answer questions of disobedience because the Church was in effect saying that the king did not run the Church. After the king had expressed his displeasure, Melville said: 'Sir, you are God's silly vassal; there are two kings and two kingdoms in Scotland: there is King James, the head of the commonwealth; and there is Christ Jesus, the King of the Church, whose subject James the Sixth is, and of whose kingdom he is not a king, not a lord, not a head, but a member.' It was a bold statement which eventually ended up with Melville being imprisoned and then exiled.

Another example is Dietrich Bonhoeffer. He was a German Lutheran pastor and theologian who publicly stood up to Hitler and lost his life because of his brave stance. His argument was not just that Christians should not obey wicked and cruel laws – but that we must learn to speak up in the face of evil. 'Silence in the face of evil is itself evil: God will not hold us guiltless. Not to speak is to speak. Not to act is to act.'

So, the Bible does teach that we should obey the government. But it does not teach that we should obey the government in all circumstances. But when we disobey, we need to be very sure that we are doing so because the government is going against the law of the Lord, rather than just our own social/political opinions.

I don't like wearing facemasks – and if given the choice I normally don't wear one. But if the government makes it the law of the land – even though I don't agree with that law – I will obey it.

Can I make a plea to you? Most who read this will live in democracies where you have the right to be involved in the governing of your country. I would argue that it is not just a right, but it is also a responsibility. You will soon be able to vote – and you can speak, write and campaign for what is good and right. It is also a command of God that we should pray for those who are in power (1 Timothy 2:1-4). It is for our good, and for the good of our neighbours that we have societies that are just, peaceful and well run. Each of us has our own small part to play.

CONSIDER: Can you think of a circumstance where you would have to disobey a government law? Or one where you should obey even if you don't like it? What do you think you could do to be a better citizen of your country?

RECOMMENDED FURTHER READING:
Church and State; Good Neighbours and Good Friends – essay in *Crown Him Lord of All.*
What is the Relationship between Church and State? – R.C. Sproul
Dietrich Bonhoeffer – A Spoke in the Wheel – Dayspring MacLeod.

PRAYER: Lord God, you command us to pray for kings and those in authority. We pray for our political leaders. We ask that they would come to see that they are your servants. That you would grant them wisdom to govern justly. Enable us to be better citizens and give us the wisdom to know when we have to disobey, and the courage to stand for your Word, in Jesus name. Amen.

10. EDUCATION AND FAITH

BIBLE READING: Colossians 2:1-5

TEXT: 'My goal is that they may be encouraged in heart and united in love, so that they may have the full riches of complete understanding, in order that they may know the mystery of God, namely, Christ, in whom are hidden all the treasures of wisdom and knowledge' (Colossians 2:2-3).

There is a very strange belief that many people have in our society. We think that we are cleverer, and more intelligent than our ancestors. We have this unreasonable belief that each generation is smarter than the next – because we are 'progressing'. But that is a blind faith – which has little evidence to support it.

As regards belief in God – the assumption is made that when human beings evolved and came out of the swamp and became conscious (incidentally the really intelligent people cannot tell us how consciousness came about) – we looked up at the sun and thought it was a god and we should worship it. Again, they don't tell us how we came up with the idea of gods and worship. They argue that humans first of all became polytheists (worshipping trees, stars and animals as gods); then, as we became more intelligent, we became monotheists (believing only in one God); and nowadays the really intelligent people just go one step further and believe that there is no God.

This is a myth. One which is not particularly intelligent. The fact that lots of people who have been educated believe it, does not make it any more reasonable or rational. Do you remember the story of the emperor's new clothes? The emperor was persuaded by a tailor that he could make him a grand set of clothes which could only be seen by the really intelligent. When this invisible set of (non-existent) clothes was put on, everyone wanted to appear intelligent and so they commented about how grand and beautiful they were. Until one small boy shouted out in the crowd 'the emperor is naked. He has no clothes'! And then the truth became obvious to everyone.

In today's society there are people who will tell you that intelligent people don't believe in God. So, if you want to appear intelligent you will say you don't believe in God. I remember being ridiculed in school – by my fellow pupils as well as a couple of teachers – when I came to believe and trust in Jesus. I had tried really hard to be an atheist – but the trouble was that it just did not make sense to me. How could everything come from nothing? Where do we get good and evil from? Why do human beings have a desire to worship? Atheism was just too dumb for me! Philosophy, art, ethics, history and even science all pointed to God – not away from him! (See *ASK* 8 for the question about science).

It also depends what you mean by education. When education was based upon Christian principles, pupils and students were taught how to think – not what to think. But nowadays much education is more about telling us what to think – making sure we have the 'right' opinions and views. It is more social engineering and indoctrination than it is education. In fact, I would go so far as to say that the more indoctrinated you are, the less likely you are to believe – but once you start questioning, thinking for yourself and seeking you are far more likely to believe.

When I tried to be an atheist, I sometimes had the view that Christians were less well educated. But then I kept meeting Christians who were very well educated (and I also met a lot of atheists who, to say the least, were not wise!). One of these is Greg Sheridan, the foreign editor of an Australian newspaper. He is a really intelligent man – and has written a wonderful book about Jesus – and some of his followers today – who are intelligent, reasonable and compassionate people.

You don't have to have a formal education to believe or disbelieve. Although if you are indoctrinated in an atheist system you are much more likely to be an unbeliever. But please don't make the mistake of attributing that to intelligence!

Being educated is not the same as being wise. For that you need Christ 'in whom are hidden all the treasures of wisdom and knowledge'. My prayer is that you will become wise!

CONSIDER: Why do you think that some people associate belief in God with being 'uneducated'? What harm can education do? What good can it do? What would make a good education?

RECOMMENDED FURTHER READING:

Christians – The Urgent Case for Jesus in our World – Greg Sheridan.

PRAYER: Lord Jesus, you are the source of all wisdom and knowledge. By you the whole earth was created. If we want to be wise, we will know you. Lord, grant us that wisdom. Open the eyes of the blind and help us all to see your glory. Amen.

11. POST-TRUTH

BIBLE READING: John 18:28-40

TEXT: 'What is truth?' retorted Pilate (John 18:38).

When you are a child things are simple. You believe what your parents tell you. You believe what your teacher tells you. You believe what anyone tells you. But very quickly you learn how dangerous that can be. We observe with the Psalmist that 'everyone is a liar' (Psalm 116:11). We become the victim of lies and the teller of lies. We know that truth is important but the more we go on, the harder we find it to know what the truth is. In fact, we now live in a world where what is called objective truth (that is real truth – things that are really true) is denied. Instead, we are left to just make up our own truth. In the words of the Manic Street Preachers, 'this is my truth, tell me yours'. It is a very confusing world. A world of spin, social media and fake news. Is it true that we have moved beyond true truth and now just live in a world where we can make up our own?

There are those who argue that in this post-truth world, all truth depends on power. The people who decide what is true are the powerful. They are the oppressors. There is a certain amount of truth in that – but it is not the whole truth.

Let's look at what the Bible has to say about truth. It is the devil who is the father of lies – and who introduced humanity to falsehood – claiming that if we disobeyed God we would be like God. (Genesis 3). This has always been humanities biggest problem. We exchange the truth of God for a lie – we worship and serve the created thing, rather than the Creator (Romans 1:25). Jesus tells us 'I am the way, the truth and the life' (John 14:6). When we reject him, we are rejecting truth.

So, in that sense – much of the Western world is now rejecting its Christian foundations – and is choosing to live by lies. In a world which believes that truth is determined by power, those who get power seek to rewrite the truth. That is why we now have a world where powerful people cannot tell us what a woman is. A world where words have less and less meaning. Where language is used in an Orwellian way.

George Orwell wrote one of the most important books of the twentieth-century – 1984. In this book about a dystopian future, he spoke prophetically about how truth could be distorted by The Party. 'War is peace; Freedom is slavery; Ignorance is strength'. 'It's a beautiful thing, the destruction of words.' You will notice how in our culture the meaning of words is being destroyed. Just think of how equality now means inequality, tolerance means intolerance and diversity means uniformity.

Orwell recognised that if you controlled education and the media you could rewrite history 'And if all others accepted the lie which the Party imposed—if all records told the same tale—then the lie passed into history and became truth.' 'Who controls the past' ran the Party slogan, 'controls the future: who controls the present controls the past.'

But he holds out the possibility of something different. 'There was truth and there was untruth, and if you clung to the truth even against the whole world, you were not mad.'

But we need to be careful here. Sometimes we can just exchange one lie for another. The internet is full of conspiracy theories and many false facts. That's another way the devil distorts the truth - sowing confusion and uncertainty.

There is also the danger that we just accept truths we like - and deny or avoid the truths we do not like.

So, can we overcome all of that? The answer is straightforward. Pilate tried to avoid the question of the truth of Jesus being innocent by asking 'what is truth'? The implication is that we could not know. We might as well just give up the search for truth. But that itself is not true.

We can know the truth, because ultimately the truth is found in a person - Jesus Christ. He is the fountain and source of all truth. All truth is God's truth.

The post-truth world is a world that is on a highway to hell. Those who walk in the truth of Christ are on the way to heaven - and will experience a foretaste of that joy, love and beauty on earth. Know the truth and the truth will set you free.

CONSIDER: How to find out whether something is true or not? What role does humility play? How does relying on Jesus as the truth, help you see more clearly the truth?

RECOMMENDED FURTHER READING:
Live not by Lies – Rod Dreher
1984 – George Orwell

PRAYER: O Lord, send forth your light and truth; let them be guides to me. Open my eyes that I may see clearly. Set me free by your truth. Lord Jesus, I believe in you. Grant me the wisdom to see all things in your light, for your glory. Amen.

12. BEING A CHRISTIAN SOLDIER

QUESTION: Can a Christian also become a soldier and kill people and yet the Bible says, 'Do not kill?'

BIBLE READING: Acts 10:1-48

TEXT: The men replied, 'We have come from Cornelius the centurion. He is a righteous and God-fearing man, who is respected by all the Jewish people. A holy angel told him to ask you to come to his house so that he could hear what you have to say' (Acts 10:22).

In the Second World War my grandad was a 'conscientious objector'. In other words, he refused to go and fight because of his objections as a Christian. He wanted Hitler to be defeated so he played his part by allowing his farm to be used as a prisoner of war camp. German prisoners came and stayed there – none of them escaped – why would they? Who would want to leave a farm in the Scottish borders to go and fight on the Eastern Front?!

There has been a long tradition of Christian pacifism. Some argue on the basis of verses such as Micah 4:3, 'they will beat their swords into ploughshares, and their spears into pruning hooks. Nation will not take up sword against nation, nor will they train for war anymore', and Matthew 5:39; 'Do not resist an evil person. If anyone slaps you on the right cheek, turn to them the other cheek also'. If we are to love our enemies – how does becoming a soldier and perhaps killing them fit in?

Yet there is another side to this. We live in a fallen and imperfect world. What if someone came into your school and started shooting all the children – would the police be justified in shooting the shooter? What if a country like Russia invaded Ukraine? Would the Ukrainians have a right to defend themselves? Do Christians have a right to be policemen or soldiers?

In Acts 10 we are told about a Roman soldier, Cornelius the centurion (literally meant he was in charge of 100 troops) who is described as 'righteous and God-fearing'. So, it is possible to be in the army and be righteous and God-fearing. There is no indication that when Cornelius became a Christian, he stopped being a soldier. Theodoret, one of the early church fathers wrote of the Emperor Diocletian that he 'made an edict ordering the Galileans (his nickname for Christians) to be expelled from the army' – showing that Christians were in the army.

You state that the Bible says, 'do not kill'. But the sixth commandment is more accurately translated 'do not murder'. (Exodus 20:13). Murder is unjust killing – the taking of an innocent human life. But there can be such a thing as just killing.

Paul tells the Roman Christians that the State authorities 'bear the sword' because they are 'God's servants, agents of wrath to bring punishment on the wrongdoers' (Romans 13:1-7). Nowhere is a Christian forbidden from being a servant for the State.

But what about war? Especially in today's world – surely that cannot be right? Augustine was a great African Christian teacher from the fourth-century. He developed what has been called 'Just War Theory'. He argued that there would always be wars, and that wars were sinful. If any Christian was involved in a war it had to be with sadness. Sin was the cause of war, but war could be a cure for sin. A state could fight a war in order to maintain peace. 'True religion looks upon as peaceful those wars that are waged not for motives of aggrandisement, or cruelty, but with the object of securing peace, of punishing evil-doers, and of uplifting the good'.

The seventeenth-century Dutch Christian philosopher Hugo Grotius developed Augustine's just war theory. For a war to be just it must

1. have a just cause (just seeking to grab more land would not be a just cause),
2. be a last resort,
3. be declared by a proper authority,
4. possess right intention,
5. have a reasonable chance of success, and
6. the end must be proportionate to the means used (i.e. you would not drop a nuclear bomb on Moscow if you want to get Crimea back for the Ukraine!).

This is a difficult subject, and it is not always easy to work out where the dividing law between good and evil falls (except as

Solzhenitsyn pointed out through the middle of every human heart!). In my view a Christian should err towards pacifism, and only take part in war reluctantly, if it is justified and necessary. The Lord hates violence, but sometimes it is necessary to restrain evil and prevent further violence – until the day the Lord returns. Meanwhile we pray that he will make wars to cease and breaks the bow and shatters the spear (Psalm 46:9).

CONSIDER: When do you think a war is unjust? Should a Christian soldier obey an unjust or evil command?

RECOMMENDED FURTHER READING:
Issues Facing Christians Today – 4th Edition – John Stott
Just War Theory Isn't Obsolete – Gregory Brown –
https://www.thepublicdiscourse.com/2016/04/16772/

PRAYER: Lord Jesus Christ, you are the Prince of Peace, yet you are also the warrior who brings justice on the earth. We know that violence and destruction are not your desire for those made in your image. May we be blessed by having peace, and by being peacemakers. Come soon and end all war, Amen.

15. THE GOOD LIE

BIBLE READING: Joshua 2

TEXT: 'By faith the prostitute Rahab, because she welcomed the spies, was not killed with those who are disobedient' (Hebrews 11:31).

First, we need to remember what lying is. The dictionary definition is helpful – 'to make an untrue statement with intent to deceive'. Sometimes we are far too quick to accuse people of lying. On social media someone might say something that is false – temperatures in the world have risen by 10 per cent – without telling a lie. They read it somewhere and have passed it on as fact. It is wrong – but not a lie. Nonetheless we should try to make sure we get our facts right!

But deliberately telling falsehoods – seeking to deceive someone is wrong. It is the devil who is the father of lies. The ninth commandment tells us not to bear false witness; Proverbs 6:16-19 warns us that the Lord hates a lying tongue and a false witness who pours out lies; Jesus is the truth, and he wants his disciples to speak the truth.

We live in a world where the devastation of lies is seen all the time. We don't like it when politicians, shop traders, family or friends lie – yet we ourselves are guilty of it many times. We teach our children that it is important to tell the truth.

One of the most famous stories about the importance of truth telling is that of George Washington. As a six-year-old he accidentally damaged his father's cherry tree. When confronted with this he responded, 'I can't tell a lie, Pa. You know I can't tell a lie. I did cut it with my hatchet.' His father was delighted with his honesty and ever since that story has been used as an example. The irony is that the story itself is almost certainly a lie. It was made up by Mason Locke Weems who wrote a biography entitled *The Life and Memorable Actions of George Washington*. It was only in its sixth edition that he added this story. Weems was trying to present Washington as a model citizen. It is ironic that in order to present the importance of telling the truth, Weems used a story that was a lie! As a clergyman he should have known better!

So, we know that lying is wrong and that we should always seek to be honest and tell the truth. But are there exceptions? In a fallen world I think we have to say yes. There are two instances in the Bible where people are commended even though their actions involved lying. The Hebrew midwives told Pharaoh a lie about why they could not kill the Hebrew babies and the Lord rewarded them for it (Exodus 1:15-21). Then in Joshua 2, Rahab lied about the Israelite spies – yet as Hebrews 11:31 points out, she was commended for her faith in doing this! You could argue that in these examples people were not commended for lying – but they were commended for their actions – of which lying was the key part!

An obvious modern example is that of Corrie ten Boom. Have you read her story – *The Hiding Place*? I would strongly recommend you do so. Corrie and her family hid Jews in their home in the Netherlands during the second world war. When the Nazis knocked on the door and asked them if they had any Jews in the house – should they have said 'I cannot tell a lie – they are upstairs in the loft?' Even keeping silent would have been an answer.

I would certainly argue that in very rare circumstances lying might be the right thing to do. But remember that good exceptions made bad laws. Such is the world that we live in that we will sometimes find ourselves in the situation where the only options seem bad ones – and we are compelled to choose the lesser of two evils. In the case you cite – we know that lying is wrong – but so would giving up your parents to be killed – so what should you do?

The situation you describe is highly implausible. Would it not be better to shout out to your parents to warn them – rather than tell a lie which the gunman is highly unlikely to believe anyway? But if, somehow, the only option was telling a lie and saving your parents or telling the truth and killing them – then I don't believe the first would be a sin. I very much doubt that you will ever be in a situation where the only good alternative is to tell a lie.

Our motto should always be – 'speak the truth in love' (Ephesians 4:15).

CONSIDER: Have you ever told a lie that was good or necessary? Have you ever told a lie which you thought was good or necessary, but then it turned out to be wrong?

RECOMMENDED FURTHER READING:
The Hiding Place – Corrie ten Boom

PRAYER: Lord, you are the God of all truth. And we keep on living, telling and enabling lies. Have mercy on us. Enable us to speak the truth in love. Grant that we may live honest lives – seeking to bring light into a dark world. May we never use bad means to try and achieve good ends – but help us to live by faith in you. Amen.

QUESTION: Why is my family not Christian?

BIBLE READING: 1 Corinthians 7:10-24

TEXT: 'How do you know, wife, whether you will save your husband? Or, how do you know husband, whether you will save your wife?' (1 Corinthians 7:16).

We want the best for the people we love – and the best is for them to come to know Christ. Some people are brought up in a Christian home and come to share the faith of their parents (some of course reject that faith). But others are brought up in a non-Christian home, who become believers and then their parents or siblings follow them.

I don't know your personal circumstances – and all of us have different ones – and there are many reasons why people are not Christians. Some have rejected the truth but others have not heard it – yet. The question 'why are my family not

Christians?' is not the most important one. The vital issue is that they become Christians.

There may be some hostility, suspicion and resentment. Jesus warned his disciples that sometimes there would be a cost in following him. One of the greatest is when your family disown you because you have come to faith in Christ. I think of the Muslim who, after he was baptised, was rejected by his family. Or the Chinese woman who was concerned about the impact on her parents of her going against the family tradition and becoming a believer. Or the parents of a student who had started coming to our church in Dundee. When she wrote home telling them how much she enjoyed going to church they were so concerned that they came down to visit us to check us out. And I will never forget the moment as a teenage boy when a group of us were having a Bible study in our home – and one father stormed into the house, furious at his teenage son: 'I thought you were at an all night party and then I found out you were at one of these Bible things – go home! You're grounded!'

Jesus warned us we could expect costly opposition – 'And everyone who has left houses or brothers or sisters or father or mother or wife or children or fields for my sake will receive a hundred times as much and will inherit eternal life.' (Matthew 19:29). But we never give up on our families – and Christ will never give up on us.

But your family may be more apathetic and tolerant. They don't really care what religious views you have – as long as you don't really change. If you do your school work, homework and don't take your religion too seriously – they might just let you be – regarding it more like your taste in music or your support of a particular football team.

The most wonderful thing is when your family respond positively to your becoming a Christian. They are intrigued by the change, pleased at the improvement in your behaviour and delighted at your joy. They might even think that they should investigate Christianity for themselves.

Which is where you come in. Before there was no Christian presence in your family – now there is. That is both a great opportunity and a great responsibility. Your family know you better than anyone else – so they will be able to observe how much your life has changed. They will be wondering if this is just a phase you are going through – and if you are really for real.

It would not be wise to preach at your family. Or to seek to 'evangelise' them – if by 'evangelise' we mean present them with a Gospel programme, or try to get them to sign up to your church. Instead we should follow the advice of Peter – 'But in your hearts revere Christ as Lord. Always be prepared to give an answer to everyone who asks you to give the reason for the hope that you have. But do this with gentleness and respect,' (1 Peter 3:15). Your life will cause them to ask questions. And you must be ready to give answers.

That is why you should study the Word, pray and continue in fellowship with your fellow believers. And it is why you should in your hearts 'revere Christ as Lord'. When you grow in your relationship with the Lord, Christ has come into your home. It is not up to you to convert your family, it is up to you to live for Christ in the hardest place of all – your home. It is up to them to respond.

CONSIDER: How do you think being a Christian has made a difference to how you treat your family? What is the best way to witness to Christ in your home? Are you faithful in prayer for those you love?

RECOMMENDED FURTHER READING:
Do Hard Things: A Teenage Rebellion Against Low Expectations – Alex and Brett Harris

PRAYER: Lord Jesus, I bless you that you have called me to yourself. I plead with you to bring my family as well – just as you have brought whole families in the past. It breaks my heart to think that they might not be with us in heaven – Lord, have mercy. Amen.

IS EUTHANASIA

QUESTION: Why can't terminally ill people be killed and put out of their misery? We do it for pets, why not humans?

BIBLE READING: Revelation 21:1-4

TEXT: 'He will wipe away every tear from their eyes. There will be no more death or mourning or crying or pain, for the old order of things has passed away' (Revelation 21:4).

A generation ago, murder was rare, abortion was illegal and euthanasia and physician–assisted suicide was unthinkable. Now murder is frequent, abortion is 'normal' and euthanasia and physician assisted suicide is legal in some places.' (Kieran Beville)

There has been an enormous change in public ethics in the Western world in the past few decades. These changes continue. As we move away from Christian foundations we are regressing to a Greco/Roman pagan view of the world, rather than progressing to a new utopia.

Euthanasia is one of those issues. Given the way our society thinks and the way that the case for euthanasia is put forward (even changing the name to physician assisted suicide or other such euphemisms as 'dignity in dying'), it is little wonder that young people especially find the case compelling.

A pastor went into a university in Scotland to take part in a debate on this subject. He was up against it. The motion was worded in his opponent's favour – who was in turn a government expert on the subject. In the vote before the debate the vast majority of people approved of the motion supporting euthanasia. But afterwards there had been a significant change – the numbers were almost even. One of the lecturers complained afterwards: 'This is a liberal university – I have never seen students change their minds like that – that should not happen'. It was pointed out to him that one of the reasons that so many students had changed their mind is because they had never heard the other side of the arguments.

Which is why your question is so revealing. You talk of people being put out of their misery, just as an animal can be put out of its misery. But do we really want to treat humans like dogs? I had a dog that had to be put down because it started 'sheep worrying'. It was heart-breaking. But if one of my children started doing something that was wrong, I would not suggest putting them down! We don't treat humans like animals! Now, I realise the situation is vastly different, but we are talking about the taking of human life – and all the risks that go along with that.

There is way more to this than can be dealt with in this short answer – but I would suggest you read the recommended book below. But let me offer some brief observations.

In the Second World War the Nazis ordered Dutch doctors to euthanise the disabled and others. The doctors all refused. Move forward seventy-five years and now we have Dutch doctors doing what some Nazi doctors were found guilty of in a court of law. Although the idea behind euthanasia is compassion – 'compassion' without Christ and the biblical understanding of life often leads to the Nazi idea.

Some people don't like this 'slippery slope' argument. But we see it all the time. For example, abortion was supposed to be rare, safe and limited to clearly defined circumstances such as a threat to the life of the mother. But that quickly degenerated to abortion on demand. When you give up the commandment 'you shall not kill', then you open the door to increased killing. Just look at the situation in the Netherlands where voluntary euthanasia has quickly turned into involuntary euthanasia. Doctors are now killing those whom they determine might have a lesser quality of life – without their permission. At the time of writing Canada in particular is moving towards a widening of euthanasia which is especially concerning.

Another concern is that those who talk about 'the right to die' see it as a principle of empowerment. But who is being empowered? The family who don't want to see their relatives suffer or their inheritance squandered? The doctors? The hospitals who don't want the elderly or disabled taking up valuable bed space? The drug companies?

But don't we want to care for those who are suffering? Absolutely. We need to offer great palliative care, to alleviate suffering and to pray. And remember this – each dying person has an eternal soul and is going to an eternal destiny. If we kill someone, we could be sending them to greater suffering! We want them to go to the situation described in Revelation 21. Remember that care for the person includes care for their souls. Our motto should be care not killing.

CONSIDER: How do you think we could care for the dying and suffering - other than euthanasia? What are the dangers of a society which allows euthanasia?

RECOMMENDED FURTHER READING:

There are some really helpful articles from the Christian Medical Fellowship ie. *https://www.cmf.org.uk/resources/publications/content/?context=article&id=26093*

PRAYER: O Lord, we long to be with you in the new heavens and new earth - where there will be no more death, pain, sorrow and suffering. We long for the old order of things to pass away. But meanwhile whilst we are on this earth - help us to treat people with dignity, to alleviate suffering and to proclaim you to them, in Christ's Name. Amen.

16. CHILD DEATH

BIBLE READING: 2 Samuel 12:1-25

TEXT: 'But now that he is dead, why should I go on fasting? Can I bring him back again? I will go to him, but he will not return to me' (2 Samuel 12:23).

I can only imagine the pain of someone who has carried a child for nine months – only for that child to be born dead. In my work as a pastor, it was a situation I came across several times. And is there anything more heart-rending than the little white coffin bearing the body of an eighteen-month girl who died in her cot? What about those who, having had an abortion, later realise that it was their child who was killed, and wonder what happened to her? Many parents have experienced the sorrow of miscarriage – where all the joy of expectant motherhood and fatherhood, turns to sorrow and loss?

I know of one man who talks about his six children. He only has three living, but his wife had three miscarriages. 'I will meet them in heaven'. Is he right?

What about those who die in infancy? Are they saved? There were (are) those who believed that if a child died without being baptised it would go to hell. Some Catholics believed that an unbaptised child would go to a place called Limbo. But there is no scriptural warrant for such a place – nor indeed for purgatory. As to children going to hell – I don't believe that that is what the Bible teaches.

The Bible says that the dead are judged according to what they have done (Revelation 20:12). Obviously, babies in the womb, or in early infancy have done nothing. But what about original sin? By that we mean the sinful nature which all human beings have inherited from Adam. Could we not be judged for that? Christ tells us that we are to let the little children come to him, and not to hinder them, for the kingdom of heaven belongs to such as these (Matthew 19:13-15). I believe that when Christ died on the cross, he also covered the sin of these little ones who die in infancy.

That is why in our reading King David weeps, fasts and prays as he longs for his new-born child to be restored to health. But when the child dies, instead of continuing like this – as his servants feared – he got up and stated that now he knew he would go to him, not the other way round. This is a clear indication of a belief that he would meet his child in the afterlife.

None of this is to say that we should not mourn the death of a child. It is a deep loss – one that cuts into the deepest recesses of our hearts. But there is healing. I would also argue that without God none of this sorrow and pain can make any sense. I think of the young atheist couple whose child died. The local minister was astonished to see the mother in church the following Sunday. 'Lovely to see you but why are you here?' 'IF there is no God, then none of this makes sense'. Sometimes pain drives us to God, rather than away from him.

Or I think of the farmer's wife whose two children were killed in a barn fire. A cruel 'friend' mocked 'where is your God now?' 'He is on the throne, as he always is'.

The Christian writer and Bible teacher, Nancy Guthrie, whose book I highly recommend, went through her own experience of such a deep loss – with the death of two of her children. She talks about how her belief in the goodness and sovereignty of God are a great source of comfort and strength.

'But because I believe God's plans for me are better than what I could plan for myself, rather than run away from the path he has set before me, I want to run toward it. I don't want to try to change God's mind—his thoughts are perfect. I want to think his thoughts. I don't want to change God's timing—his timing is perfect. I want the grace to accept his timing. I don't want to change God's plan—his plan is perfect. I want to embrace his plan and see how he is glorified through it. I want to submit.' Nancy Guthrie

The book of Job is a great insight into the depths of suffering that human beings can go through. But at the end all our hope is in the knowledge that 'I know that my Redeemer lives, and that in the end he will stand on the earth. And after my skin has been destroyed, yet in my flesh I will see God.' (Job 19:25-27). The resurrection is our hope.

CONSIDER: How would you comfort and help someone who has experienced the loss of a child?

RECOMMENDED FURTHER READING:
Holding On to Hope: A Pathway through Suffering to the Heart of God – Nancy Guthrie

PRAYER:
Lord Jesus, you wept at the grave of Lazarus, because you were furious at the pain of death. We praise your name that you came to defeat death. O Lord, grant your comfort to those who have experienced the loss of their precious little ones. We pray that you would save and keep all those who die so young. You are our merciful Saviour. Amen.

17. AND IT WAS SO ...

BIBLE READING: Genesis 1

TEXT: 'God saw all that he had made, and it was very good. And there was evening, and there was morning - the sixth day' (Genesis 1:31).

You are referring to Genesis chapter 1 where 'and it was so' is stated after God commands that the waters be separated (v. 7), the dry ground appear (v. 9), the land produce vegetation (v. 11), the sun, moon and stars be lights (v. 15), the wild and domestic animals be created (v. 24) and that mankind be created as the ruler of the earth (v. 28). This tells us one simple truth - that God spoke and when he spoke it happened. Sometimes we can say things, command things, or promise things – and they don't happen. But God spoke and it came into being.

We now know that every living thing consists of information. You and I for example have a unique DNA – that if stretched out, could go all the way to the moon and back! It's just a combination of four letters A, C, G and T. God spoke the world into being. The Word (Logos) created everything by the word of his power.

Then after each act of creation we see that God says, 'it was good'. It is not just that God created but that everything he created was good. But notice the difference in the very last verse of chapter one. God saw that it was 'very good'. This is after the creation of humanity – the apex of God's creation. The all-powerful God created a good world.

Now that immediately causes a question to arise. Some look at the creation and see that it is not good. Like for example the well-known atheist Stephen Fry who said: 'You can't just say there is a God because well, the world is beautiful. You have to account for bone cancer in children. You have to account for the fact that almost all animals in the wild live under stress with not enough to eat and will die violent and bloody deaths. There is not any way that you can just choose the nice bits and say that means there is a God and ignore the true fact of what nature is.'

Does he not have a point? Yes – but it is a very limited one – and is in fact answered by your question. If there was no God we would just be left with nature 'red in tooth and claw', evil and pain – and there would be no explanation and very little we could do about it. However, the Bible goes further than Fry's somewhat simplistic analysis. It tells us that the all-powerful

God, did create a good world, but that there was the Fall which affected and infected everything. What do we mean by the Fall?

Humanity was created as the apex of God's creation. Male and female were both made in his image. We were then given the choice to believe, obey and serve God freely. We chose not to. And as a result, evil entered into the world and, amongst other things, the earth was cursed (Genesis 3:17). So, when Fry and others complain that God did not create the world good, they are not telling the truth. The problem is that Fry does not accept that there is a God at all, never mind a good God. Even more they do not accept that there is such a thing as sin - or at least personal sin which they, like every human being, has. And they have no hope for the future of the planet or the universe. Romans 8 tells us that the whole creation is groaning, waiting for the children of God to be revealed - so that it can be released from its bondage to decay. Stephen Fry and others have no answer nor any hope. Christ does. God brought the world into being by the power of his Word - and he will rescue it by the power of the Word!

So, you see that these two phrases are really important. They tell us of an all-powerful creator and of the fact that God is good and that this good God created a good earth. The alternative is hellish and hopeless.

CONSIDER: What hope is there if we live in a world which is fundamentally bad? What hope is there for a world if there is no good God? Why should the goodness of God give you great hope?

RECOMMENDED FURTHER READING:

Genesis 1-4 - In the Beginning - Roger Fawcett

PRAYER: Lord our God, you are good and the giver of all things good. All you created was good. We know that in your providence you permitted humanity to turn away from you and spoil your good creation. Yet we also know that you have determined to save and renew – and you have promised that all things work for the good of those who love you. We love you and praise your name! Amen.

16. BIBLE MISTAKES

BIBLE READING: Psalm 119:153-160

TEXT: 'All your words are true; all your righteous laws are eternal' (Psalm 119:160).

The young man was adamant. 'The Bible's rubbish ... it's full of mistakes. 'Have you read the Bible?' 'No'. Discussion over!

Sometimes people argue that the Bible is full of contradictions – and yet when you ask them to name one, they really struggle. It's just something that 'everyone' knows. But often what people assume to be obvious, turns out not to be obvious. And that is certainly the case with this myth.

There are people who have read the Bible and who have found apparent contradictions in the Bible. But note the word 'apparent.' On closer examination you usually find that the case is not as clear cut as they assume. In *ASK* chapters two and three we looked at how we can trust the Bible as God's unchanging Word. Now we are looking at the 'mistakes.'

If you are asking this question because it is causing you problems in your faith, or holding you back from believing, I feel your pain! Not long after I became a Christian, when I was about sixteen years old, someone gave me a book which I think was entitled *101 difficulties in the Bible – answered*. As a young newly born Christian I had had no difficulties with the Bible. After I read that book, I had 101! Because the problems were real, but I didn't find the answers satisfying or helpful. And to be honest it gave me a real crisis of faith. After praying about it, the thought struck me – why shouldn't parts of the Bible be difficult? Why should I expect to understand it all? After all I am just a baby Christian. I don't have to know everything at once. God will surely teach you as you go along.

And over the years that is exactly what has happened. I thought 'let God be true and every man a liar' (Romans 3:4). Perhaps of those 101 difficulties I am now down to about four or five. I have slowly learned that whilst it is not wrong to question and think – it is wrong for me to sit in judgement upon the Word of God as though I am its master and I know all things.

Psalm 119 is the longest chapter in the Bible – and it is about the Bible. It is one of the most amazing chapters you will read. In fact, it will repay you enormously if you read it slowly, even memorise it and meditate upon it. The reading for this chapter (vv. 153-160) tells us a great deal about God's Word. It is not something we should forget; it is a promise to preserve our lives; we are to hold on to God's statutes; the faithless are those who do not obey God's Word; and we are to love God's precepts.

But the verse I want you to hold on to is simply v. 160 'All your words are true; all your righteous laws are eternal'.

Think about what that means. And how wonderful it is. Is there anyone else of whom you can say 'all your words are true'? We can get truth from many different people - but there is no person on earth of whom we can say 'you are the truth, you always speak the truth, to know you is to know truth'. Isn't that the beauty of Jesus? He never lies to us. His Word never fails.

I don't know what country you live in. But I do know that the laws keep on changing. If we live in Western liberal democracies, we accept the rule of law - and the fact that we expect laws to be just and fair. But we also know that laws keep changing - that they are not always righteous, and they are certainly not eternal. There are things now that are illegal which were once law - and vice versa. It is only God's law that is righteous and is eternal.

That is why it is not full of mistakes. Does God speak error? Of course not! To even suggest such a thing is to believe the first lie of the devil when he asked Eve 'Did God really say?' (Genesis 3:1).

This does not mean that copyists or translators cannot make mistakes. There is for example the infamous case of the so-called Wicked Bible where the printers left out the word 'not' from the seventh commandment so that it read 'thou shalt commit adultery'! Of course, such mistakes are easily corrected. But when we are talking about the original Scriptures - they are without error. You can bank your eternal life on it!

CONSIDER: What would you do if you came across part of the Bible that seemed to be a mistake? Or that seemed to contradict another part? How can you be assured that the Bible is without error??

RECOMMENDED FURTHER READING:
Unbreakable – What the Son of God said About the Word of God – Andrew Wilson

PRAYER: Lord God, we bless you that you are the God who speaks. And that you have given us the word of the prophets made more certain. That men spoke from you as they were carried along and inspired by your Spirit. We bless you that every word from your mouth is true. Teach us to trust, experience and know the power of that. In your Name, Amen.

19. OTHER HOLY BOOKS

QUESTION: Why is the Bible different from other sacred texts? What makes Christianity different from every other religion?

BIBLE READING: 2 Peter 1:12-21

TEXT: 'For we did not follow cleverly devised stories when we told you about the coming of our Lord Jesus Christ in power, but we were eyewitnesses of his majesty' (2 Peter 1:16).

Do you ever notice the air you breath? No? That's because it's so much part of our lives that we rarely think about it. That is true of the cultural air that we breath – the beliefs and ideas that our society is based upon. One such idea is that all religions are fundamentally the same. If you stop and think about it that doesn't really make sense. But the trouble is that we just don't stop and think about the air we breathe.

So, when some one suggests that it is arrogant or wrong to say that the Bible is 'different' with the implication being that it is better, than other religious texts, that just feels wrong. And yet we must not go by our feelings. We should read and think for ourselves.

The first thing to say is that there is truth in other holy books. When the Buddha says 'radiate boundless love towards the entire world' – it's not wrong. Although it is impossible – only Christ does that! When the Hindu Scriptures teach 'A gift is pure when it is given from the heart to the right person at the right time and at the right place, and when we expect nothing in return' they are not saying something that is wrong. Although again in this quote we just simply ask whether anything can be pure from impure humans! These 'scriptures' may give us profound ideas and beautiful concepts but ultimately they don't help us, because they don't give us Christ.

After a debate in a Scottish university a young woman in a burka approached me and asked this question: 'David, do you really believe that there is one God, that he is the Creator of heaven and earth, that he is sovereign and that there is heaven and hell?' 'Yes – I do.' 'Well, you are a very unusual Christian – you are almost a Muslim!' I'm not sure about the 'Christians' she had met, but she was right in noting the similarities. But it is the differences which are even greater. The Qur'an teaches that it is blasphemy to speak of Jesus Christ as God. The Bible says it is essential for salvation.

How do we know what is right? There is a Confession of Faith from the seventeenth-century, the Westminster Confession (one that is still used by many churches today), which expresses it beautifully. I suggest you get a copy and read chapter 1 – but especially part 5. It argues that good reasons for believing that the Bible is the Word of God, include the testimony of the Church; the beauty of the style; the fact that the doctrine works; the unity of all the parts; the scope of the whole – giving glory to God; the full discovery it gives of the way of salvation; and many other excellencies and perfection. However, it points out that this is not enough – we need the 'inward work of the Holy Spirit, bearing witness by and with the word in our hearts', in order for us to be fully persuaded of its infallible truth.

That's why I simply suggest that you read the Bible prayer-fully, asking God to enlighten and open your mind and heart. In reading other 'sacred' texts I have found my faith in the Bible as God's Word being greatly strengthened. Why? Because when I read the Qur'an, or the Buddhist or Hindu scriptures, or the book of Mormon; and then contrast them with the Bible there is no contest. They are as different as chalk and cheese!

The reason is straightforward. Every religion is an attempt by human beings to reach up to God. In biblical Christianity it is the other way round. God reaches down to us. He does that primarily through Jesus Christ – but how would we know Christ without the Scriptures? God has sent his Spirit to give us his Word, that we may receive his Son. It's simple, profound and beautiful.

CONSIDER: If the Bible is God's Word given to reveal Himself and his plan of salvation, why would we neglect it? It may be good to read other things, but they should be measured according to the Word of God. Can they be considered 'sacred' or 'holy' if they are not inspired by the Holy Spirit?

RECOMMENDED FURTHER READING:

ASK 35 looked at the question of Islam.
Where to Start with Islam – Samuel Green
Engaging with Hindus – Robin Thomson

PRAYER: Lord Jesus, we thank you that we are not left to follow cleverly invented stories, or our own imaginations, but that you have given us witnesses who saw your majesty. And we bless you that you sent the Holy Spirit to remind them of everything you had taught them. We praise you Lord that everything necessary for our salvation is given to us, by you, in your Word. Hallelujah!

20. GOD AND SWEARING

BIBLE READING: Ephesians 4:29– 5:7

TEXT: 'Nor should there be obscenity, foolish talk or coarse joking, which are out of place, but rather thanksgiving' (Ephesians 5:4).

What is swearing? One definition is 'to make a statement or promise with an oath'. I presume that you are not really asking about that. If you were then we would be discussing James 5:12: 'Above all, my brothers and sisters, do not swear – not by heaven or earth or by anything else. All you need to say is a simple "Yes" or "No". Otherwise, you will be condemned.' That would be a whole other discussion.

In this question we are talking about swearing as 'bad or vulgar language'. It seems to be something that is increasingly common in our everyday lives. Words that you would not have heard on daytime TV are now commonplace on mainstream media. Words that would rarely be heard outside a drinking den are now often used around the family table! In Australia, where I live, I have been quite surprised at how common swearing and profanity is in everyday conversation – even amongst Christians.

When my youngest daughter was about eight years old, we went to that citadel of fine football, Dens Park, the home of Dundee F. C. You always expect bad language at a football game – whether an individual shouting in frustration (a common experience as a Dundee fan!), or a collective chant. But this particular Saturday was especially bad. A group of young men behind us were swearing and shouting non-stop. It was so irritating that I was preparing to move when another young man in front of us, stood up, turned round and shouted to his fellow supporters: "You'se … shut up … stop that xxxxx swearing. Can't you see that there is an XXXX wee lassie here and she doesn't need to hear that kind of XXXX language!' He then went on to berate them in similar vein for a couple of minutes – before realising that he was swearing at his colleagues for swearing! He then turned to me and said 'sorry, mate!' I couldn't stop laughing.

What is wrong with swearing?

Let's consider the different types. There is a form of mild swearing – even to the extent of using substitute swear words like 'sugar'. I suppose that if you struggle with having the vocabulary to express your feelings, then you can see a justification for using such.

Then there is blasphemy. Many people see this as being a form of mild swearing. Using God's name (i.e., 'O God' or 'for

God's sake') is a norm amongst young and old, rich and poor. What astounds me is how often Christians fall into this habit. What's wrong with it? It's blasphemy. 'You shall not misuse the name of the Lord your God, for the LORD will not hold anyone guiltless who misuses his name.' (Exodus 20:7). God's Name is holy. His Name is blessed. His Name is pure. His Name reveals who he is. We don't go as far as the Jews who regarded 'the Name' as so sacred that they would not even say it. But to go to the other extreme of using 'the Name' as a swear word, or even some kind of spiritual punctuation is appalling.

A friend and I were playing football in an amateur team in the village of Brora, in the Scottish Highlands. One of our teammates kept using the name of Jesus as a swear word. My friend eventually put his arm round him and said: 'If we used your mother's name as a swear word would you be happy? No? Well, we know Jesus – and he is more precious to us than anyone else. Could you just use another swear word – and not his name'. The young man was astonished. He told us that he wasn't using his normal sexual expletives because he didn't want to offend us – and thought we would approve of Jesus!

Another common form of swearing is using sexual words. I'm not sure why this is so popular. But the effect is to take something beautiful that God has given us and turn it in to something ugly. The trouble is that once an ugly swear word which is rarely used becomes commonplace, people then look for even uglier words to shock, mock and attack.

This is where Paul's warning to the Ephesians comes in. Christians should avoid obscenity, foolish talk and coarse joking.

We will often find this hard. The tongue is a 'restless evil, full of deadly poison' (James 3:8). No one can tame it. But with the aid of the Spirit, and his gift of self –control, it is possible. Let's make sure that praise, words that build up, words of beauty and words that bless are what come out of our mouths – not ugly, abusive and destructive words.

CONSIDER: If your speech is 'seasoned with salt' (Colossians 4:6), and you don't join in the dirty jokes or mocking, racist and abusive language of those around you – what impact do you think it will have? Without ever saying a word about Christ – you will show that there is something different. Let us all labour to make our speech something beautiful.

RECOMMENDED FURTHER READING:
Sinful Speech – Sins of the Tongue – John Flavel

PRAYER: 'May these words of my mouth and this meditation of my heart be pleasing in your sight, LORD, my Rock and my Redeemer' (Psalm 19:14).

21. THE BOOK OF JOB

BIBLE READING: Job 1

TEXT: 'At this, Job got up and tore his robe and shaved his head. Then he fell to the ground in worship and said:
 'Naked I came from my mother's womb,
and naked I will depart.
The LORD gave and the LORD has taken away.
may the name of the LORD be praised.'
In all this, Job did not sin by charging God with wrongdoing.'
(Job 1:20-22).

What an interesting question! In some ways it ties in with question 16 – because it is all about suffering.

The poet John Milton wrote an extraordinary poem – one of the greatest ever written in English – called *Paradise Lost*. In it he said that his purpose was 'to justify the ways of God to men'. You have asked me to justify the book of Job – possibly the greatest poem ever written in any language. Why is it in the Bible? What does it all mean? In one way it seems a really horrible story – and yet in another way it deals with exactly the same subject that Milton was writing about – the relationship between God and suffering.

I have preached through the whole book of Job – twice. The first time I did it I wasn't sure how I could. Would it not be a bit heavy for people? After all it is forty-two chapters of death, megadeath and more death! It just seems so miserable. And yet I have never had a greater response from ordinary people, than I had for this book. Why? Because it's a book that deals with the realities of life, and the questions we all have. And it does so in a deep and intense way.

When we were in the midst of Covid and not able to get out much I recorded a series of short five minute talks called 'Coffee with Job' on YouTube. We ended up doing 140 of them! For many of us it was so helpful – just seeing how the Bible is applied to normal life.

And at the time of writing this I am working with a filmmaker as he seeks to bring the book of Job to the big screen. It's such a dramatic, poetic and moving story.

So, I don't feel any need to 'justify' the book of Job. It justifies itself.

But perhaps you mean – can you justify the storyline? After all Job suffers so much – and for what? Again, I don't feel that I can or have to justify that story. Because it is, admittedly in a much more intense form, the story of us all. We are all born into a world of suffering. We all suffer. And we will all die. In Disneyland it's hard to face up to that reality. But we don't live in Disneyland! We live in the real world – the world of Job.

If Job was just a book about suffering, then it might be beautiful and real – but it would still be pretty useless to those of us who suffer. Is the message of Job really 'we all suffer – just suck it up – that's your karma!'. Not at all.

The key in Job is that God asks Job deeper questions, than Job asks God. This is a poem about worshipping God, seeking answers in humility – and above all it is a book about Jesus. All the suffering of Job finds its absolute height in the suffering of Jesus Christ. Job looks for a Redeemer. Jesus is that Redeemer. Has there ever been a greater statement of real faith than this from Job in the midst of his agony?

> I know that my redeemer lives,
> and that in the end he will stand on the earth.
> And after my skin has been destroyed, yet in my flesh I will
> see God; I myself will see him with my own eyes—I, and not
> another. How my heart yearns within me!
> (Job 19:25-27).

I love the variety that there is in the Bible – the historical books, the books of the Law, the gospels, the letters, the prophets and the poetic books – Ecclesiastes, Proverbs, Song of Solomon, Psalms, and of course, the book of Job. I am so thankful that the Holy Spirit inspired this great poem – and for the enormous source of comfort, teaching, encouragement and above all revelation of the beauty of Christ, it has been. I would strongly recommend you sit down and read the whole book for yourself – meditate on it – discuss it with others. I'm pretty sure you will soon find it justifies itself.

CONSIDER: What would be missing from the Bible if the book of Job was not in it? In what ways does Job give us a picture of Christ? Will you sit down and read through this whole book?

RECOMMENDED FURTHER READING:
Job – The Wisdom of the Cross – Christopher Ash (This is a big book and it is a commentary. But don't let that put you off. But it's so brilliant and really readable. You will love it!).
Paradise Lost – John Milton

PRAYER: O Lord God, like Job we know that you can do all things and that no purpose of yours can be thwarted. Like Job we confess that too often we speak of things we do not understand and too wonderful for us to know. But we thank you that you are not a God who remains silent. You speak. You question us. And you draw us to yourself. O Lord, even through this part of your Word may we come to see your Son, in his Name we pray. Amen.

22. WHERE TO START WITH THE BIBLE

QUESTION: If I were reading the Bible for the first time, where would I start and what book would you recommend? Why do people memorise the Bible?

BIBLE READING: Psalm 119:9-16

TEXT: 'I have hidden your word in my heart that I might not sin against you' (Psalm 119:11).

When you read a book, you start at the beginning, and you read it through to the end. It seems obvious, doesn't it? But I would suggest that's not the best approach to reading the Bible. There are around 727,969 words in the Bible, 31,102 verses, 1,189 chapters and 66 books. That's a lot of reading. It's also not like a novel or a history book which follows a plot line or a historical narrative. Nor is it a puzzle book, a science textbook, or a collection of fables. The Bible was written by around forty different authors, inspired by the Holy Spirit, over a period of around 1,500 years. The sixty-six books are of different genres. There is law (the five books of Moses), history, poetry, prophecy, gospel and letter.

So where do you begin? After a particularly lively discussion in a library in Brighton, England, a young man approached me and told me that the Bible was rubbish. When I asked him if he had read it, he admitted that he hadn't. So, I challenged him to do so. He asked your question – where do I begin? I suggested that he not start in Genesis and that he should not use the King James Version. A month later I received an e-mail from him. He apologised that he had forgotten my advice, so he had just started reading from Genesis 1 in the KJV! He had reached chapter 38 and admitted that it was freaking him out because it was beginning to make sense!

Nonetheless I would still give the same advice. Find a modern English version and begin with one of the Gospels – personally I would suggest the Gospel of Luke, because then you can go on to the book of Acts which is really Luke part 2 and tells the story of the early church. Then, in no particular order I would read Genesis, the Psalms, Ecclesiastes, Isaiah, Romans and 1 John! By then you should be well on your way!

My own personal habit is to use something called the McCheyne calendar (https://www.mcheyne.info/calendar.pdf) which is a Bible reading calendar which enables you to read the whole Bible every year – the Psalms and the New Testament twice. That sounds a lot – but it is only four chapters per day. It starts with the four great beginnings of the Bible: creation (Genesis), Christ (Matthew), the Church (Acts) and the return of Israel from exile (Ezra).

There are also some basic principles to bear in mind when reading the Bible. It is the Word of God, inspired by the Spirit of God, so it's a great idea to pray and ask God to speak to you through his Word. It's also a living Word, not a dead book. You will be amazed how often this ancient book speaks right into our contemporary society and your personal needs. (That's why I am writing this book – to show how the Word gives answers to the questions of this world). But remember it's not all about you. It is primarily a book about God. It brings us Christ and it reveals the will of God to us. Sometimes the Bible is difficult, and we won't always grasp what is going on – but that's fine. You will return to it. One of the wonderful things about God's Word is that there is always more light to come out of it. One other thing to bear in mind – remember that much of the Bible is descriptive (telling us what happened), not prescriptive (telling us what should happen). It is an honest book, showing every one of its heroes as flawed. Except Christ.

But what about memorisation? Why should we do that? Who memorises things nowadays – especially when we can just Google them on our phones? But what if your battery runs out! The reason for memorising the Word of God is summed up in the word 'meditation'. When we memorise, we slow down, we stop, we think, we reflect. The Word goes deep into our minds and hearts. Without memorisation we have a tendency to skim read, and as a result we don't go deep, and we lose a lot of the value of the Word.

Let me make a confession to you. I have not always followed this advice - even as a pastor. I don't even remember if I remembered the memory verses we used to get in Sunday school. But over the past couple of years, I have started memorising chapters of the Bible - it has been the single most life transforming thing I have done. You are young - and you have a great advantage over this older man! Your mind is keen and can absorb so much more. You can fill it with trivia and garbage - or you can fill it with the eternal words of God.

CONSIDER: What do you think the value is in reading the Bible? What chapters or verses would you like to memorise? Martin Luther once said that if you are tired of the Word of God, you are tired of life. Do you agree?

RECOMMENDED FURTHER READING:
The Bible; McCheyne Calendar
My 1st Book of Memory Verses - Carine MacKenzie
A good way to remember something is to sing it! Try Colin Buchanan's Baa Baa Doo Baa Baa: The Memory Verses which will help you get Scripture into your head and heart.
https://www.desiringgod.org/articles/why-i-memorize-books-of-the-bible

PRAYER: O Lord, how can we live pure and good lives? By living according to your Word. But how can we live according to your Word if we don't know it? Lord teach me your Word. Show me your ways. Reveal to me your beauty. Help me to hide your Word in my heart, that I might not sin against you. Help me to meditate on your precepts and consider your ways. I delight in your decrees. I will not neglect your Word. Amen.

23. THE IPHONE BIBLE

QUESTION: Some people say the Bible on the phone is not a good Bible that it is fake, but the Bible in hardcopy is the real Bible: is that true? Also, is KJV the only true Bible? How did we get the Bible?

BIBLE READING: Revelation 22:18-21

TEXT: 'I warn everyone who hears the words of the prophecy of this scroll: if anyone adds anything to them, God will add to that person the plagues described in this scroll. And if anyone takes words away from this scroll of prophecy, God will take away from that person any share in the tree of life and the Holy City, which are described in this scroll' (Revelation 22:18-19).

There are pros and cons of having your Bible on your phone. I do. And it's wonderful for looking up verses, reading on the train and listening to on my headphones. However, there are disadvantages as well – the most serious of which is that we

99

all have a tendency to skim read on screen. Which is precisely the opposite of what we were talking about in the last chapter – we need to go deep into God's Word. So, I would argue that it's much better when you are doing your normal reading to have a physical copy in front of you.

As regards your question, it's important for us to understand how we got the Bible. It wasn't given to us in printed books as we now know. The printing press was only invented in Germany in the fifteenth century. The first Bible printed on it was called the Gutenberg Bible. Before that we had the Bible on manuscripts and scrolls. The story of how the Bible came down to us through thousands of manuscripts and copies is quite remarkable. I would suggest you read F.F. Bruce's *The New Testament Documents – Are They Reliable?*

The basic summary is that the Holy Spirit inspired human beings, who wrote down what happened and what he inspired in them. The Church accepted the Jewish Bible – what we now call the Old Testament – and then the writings of the apostles – who were appointed by Jesus to be his witnesses and to carry his Word. That's how we ended up with the twenty-seven books of the New Testament – the gospels, the letters and Revelation. Contrary to myths popularised by Dan Brown's *The Da Vinci Code*, it is not the case that the Church just made up the Bible in the fourth century. As the Church grew there were lots of fake gospels and letters which came into circulation. What the Church did was formally recognise those which were apostolic and from the beginning – and then excluded all the fakes.

Ironically, I think that if we had had the Internet then it would have been far easier to corrupt the original text. Hard, handwritten copies are much harder to alter. But that does not mean that the Bible you have on your phone is not the real Bible. It's quite easy for people to fake and corrupt things online - but it is also easy for you to check. So, the NIV Bible I have on my phone is exactly the same as the NIV Bible I have on my desk.

Is the King James Version the only true Bible? No. The KJV is a fine version of the Bible, but it is not the original version. It is an English translation from 1611. The Bible was written in Hebrew, Aramaic and Greek over 1,500 years earlier! The Lord did not wait until 1,500 years after Christ to send his Word to us! We must be really careful not to add to the Word of God.

But when people say this what they mean is that the KJV is the best translation based on the best manuscripts. There is a lot of argument about the manuscript traditions - but I won't bore you with that somewhat detailed and technical textual argument. Suffice it to say that most versions of the Bible are based on the same original texts. As regards translation, I would not use the KJV. Why? Because neither you nor I speak sixteenth-century English. And the language has changed a lot. We should read the Bible in what the Westminster Confession calls 'the vulgar tongue'. 'Vulgar' in sixteenth-century English does not mean rude (this is a great example of how language changes) - it just means common or normal.

If English is your mother tongue, then get a good and accurate English translation (there are many); if you speak German, Swahili, Chinese, Spanish, Swedish, Arabian or any of the other 7,100 languages in the world - then get a Bible in your own language. The Bible has been translated in full or in part into 3,324 languages - which covers about 97 per cent of all people. About 80 per cent have the Bible in full. Organisations like Wycliffe Global Alliance https://www.wycliffe.net/ are working on translating the rest. Perhaps one day you might be able to help them?!

CONSIDER: Have you ever thought how amazing it is that God's Word has come down to us intact and unchanged? Or that almost all the world's population now have access to the Word of God in their own languages? Or that modern technology makes it even easier for us to read and hear God speak to us?

RECOMMENDED FURTHER READING:

The New Testament Documents – Are They Reliable? F.F. Bruce

PRAYER: Lord, we thank you that you are the God who speaks. In the past you spoke through the prophets and many wonderous signs, but in these last days you have spoken to us by your Son. We praise your Name that Jesus is revealed to us in the Scriptures and that we have them in our own language. We pray that you would enable us to read them and to be doers as well as hearers of the Word. Keep us O Lord from adding to your Word, or taking away from it. In Christ's Name. Amen.

24. TALKING SNAKES

BIBLE READING: Genesis 3

TEXT: 'Now the serpent was more crafty than any of the wild animals the LORD God had made. He said to the woman, "Did God really say, 'You must not eat from any tree in the garden?'" (Genesis 3:1).

This is a dangerous question. Why? Because it is usually not a serious one. It is normally asked in a mocking and contemptuous tone, with the underlying meaning being 'only a fool would believe something as stupid as that'! God warns us about having such a mocking attitude and even suggests that it is pointless trying to answer the question – because the person making it, is making an accusation rather than asking a genuine question. 'Do not rebuke mockers or they will hate you; rebuke the wise and they will love you' (Proverbs 9:8).

A number of years ago I received a phone call from Kerrang – a heavy metal radio station. To be honest at first, I thought it was a joke. But no, they really did want to do an interview with me about *The Dawkins Letters*. As I listened to the sounds of Black Sabbath and Led Zeppelin before the interview, I wondered what was coming. As soon as the music stopped the D.J. came on and asked, 'hey Dave, you don't believe in a talking snake, do you?'. I knew then that I was in for a tough time! The D.J. was brilliant. He was not mocking, despite the jocular tone of the first question and we ended up having a long conversation about God, humanity, the nature of evil and the potential of salvation.

So let me assume that you are asking this question in the same spirit of genuine curiosity and that the question of the Serpent in the garden is one that really worries you. Does it make the Bible sound like one of Aesop's fables, a bit ridiculous and unbelievable? I don't think I could pretend that Genesis 3 is an easy passage to understand, or that there are no difficulties within it – but I don't see why a talking snake should be a particular difficulty.

The Bible is not presenting the world as though it were populated with talking animals – aka Disney! What is being taught here is that it was Satan, in the form of a serpent, who tempted Adam and Eve and led them astray from God. Satan is the accuser and that deceiver. He is the one who seeks to destroy. If he is the second most powerful force in the universe, then there is no difficulty in him taking the form of a serpent or speaking through a serpent.

The objection here is not a logical one – it is a philosophical one. One of belief. If you do not believe that there can be a supernatural being, whether good or bad, then you will automatically not accept any supernatural explanation. Indeed, any such explanation will automatically be dismissed as laughable. The trouble with that argument is that it is a circular and closed one. By shutting yourself off to the possibility of the supernatural, you make any discussion impossible.

Of course, the possibility does not make it certain. However, in terms of the existence of a personal evil being, I think the evidence is somewhat overwhelming. You could deny, against all the evidence, that evil actually exists (as Richard Dawkins does in *River out of Eden*, 'The universe that we observe has precisely the properties we should expect if there is, at bottom, no design, no purpose, no evil, no good, nothing but pitiless indifference.'), or you could argue, implausibly, that evil is just an impersonal force. But the biblical explanation that evil is personified in the fallen angel, the devil, makes a lot more sense to me.

So yes – I would rather believe that evil manifested itself in the form of a talking snake to tempt humanity away from God, than believe that either evil doesn't exist, or that humans are essentially good. To believe the latter takes a leap of faith that I am not prepared to make.

I've already mentioned *Paradise Lost*, (Chapter 21) but it's such a great poem that it is worth mentioning again. Milton has Satan stating, 'better to reign in hell, than to serve in heaven'. This is the ultimate lie of the evil one. That the main thing in life is for us to rule ourselves. He offers us freedom and brings us slavery. Whereas God calls us to serve – and in so doing sets us free. We can listen to the lies of the evil one and go to destruction – or we can know the truth and be set free. Who will you listen to? The Serpent or the Saviour?

CONSIDER: Why do you think that people find the story of the snake in the garden of Eden so hard to believe? How do people explain evil without the devil? Who would you trust to defeat Satan?

RECOMMENDED FURTHER READING:
Genesis – Derek Kidner
The Serpent and the Serpent Slayer – Andrew David Naselli

PRAYER: Our Father in heaven, we pray that you would deliver us from evil and not allow us to be led into temptation. We know that our enemy, the devil, goes round like a roaring lion, seeking whom he may devour. We know that he is subtle and the father of lies. Protect us from his wiles, and lead us in your truth. We rejoice that he has already been defeated. In Jesus name. Amen.

QUESTION: What can you say about 666?

BIBLE READING: Revelation 13

TEXT: 'This calls for wisdom. If anyone has insight, let him calculate the number of the beast, for it is man's number. His number is 666' (Revelation 13:18.)

Would you accept a hotel room with the number 666? When your car reaches 666 miles and crashes do you think that's a coincidence? What do you think is on channel 666 on your TV? It's possible that you may be suffering from Hexakosioihexekontahexaphobia - now there's a word you don't hear every day. It's the fear of the number 666.

In case you think it's not a real fear, there genuinely are people who won't travel on Route 666 - apparently you can get your kicks on Route 66, but Route 666 is another matter altogether. It is a road serving the Four Corners area of the U.S. (New Mexico, Nevada) and had a higher-than-average number of accidents. It has now been renamed Route 491. And then there was the infamous case of President Ronald and Nancy Reagan who in 1989 bought a new home in the Bel Air area of Los Angeles, 666 St Cloud Road. They renumbered it to 668. They too suffered from Hexakosioihexekontahexaphobia.

Many people have an awareness of the number 666 which has now passed into popular culture, because of films like *The Omen* and of course the obsession with the number in rock music. Britney Spears wearing a 666 t-shirt, Iron Maiden singing 'The Number of the Beast', Black Sabbath, Led Zeppelin have all provided plenty of material for those Christian conspiracy theorists who see rock music as the mark of the Beast, the spawn of Satan.

Others see the mark of the beast in your social insurance number, or your credit card, or an implant in your body put there by the state when you were born, or the Covid vaccine! The theories are numerous. To my mind it is a complete waste of time, energy and money spending precious time on such silly speculations. The apostle John was not writing about credit cards or Western social welfare systems. He was not writing about Barack Obama, Donald Trump, Saddam Hussein, Adolf Hitler, Napoleon or even Bill Gates. So, what did he mean?

If you were a slave, as many of John's readers would have been, then you would have been branded, like cattle. You would also have been aware of the image of Caesar on coinage, indicating that it ultimately belonged to him. The mark was all about who you belonged to. In ancient languages letters were often used for numbers. So for example, a=1, b=2, c=3 etc. A name could be represented by adding up the numbers. There is an example in Pompeii of graffiti on a wall reading, 'I love her whose name is 545.' When you transliterate Nero Caesar from Greek to Hebrew you end up with the number 666. The number of the beast is simply the number of the Roman emperor who was persecuting the Christians. This numerical code/imagery was actually quite clever for the Christians. Why? Because they could see themselves as the number above, the heavenly 777. Even better, the name Jesus in Greek transliterated into 888.

The point of Revelation 13 is not to provide twenty-first-century Western Christian authors with material to apply to our particular political circumstances – as though the Holy Spirit was recording the event before it happened. No: he is showing John firstly that the opposition is fierce, perhaps worse even than John's worse nightmare. But he is also showing him in pictorial form that the opposition is limited. The beast out of the sea was given power to wage war against God's holy people and in the opposite of Revelation 7 to rule over every tribe, language, people and nation. It's not the Lamb at the centre of the throne who is ruling; apparently it is the beast. But even in the midst of that evil John is being told it is limited. He was 'given' the authority. His time was limited (the 42 months). We are not told the reason for any of these things. But we are told that the Lord's people have to be patient and faithful. That's one of the key lessons.

The encouragement is that the sovereignty of God is always more apparent when it seems as though wickedness has reached its deepest limit. There is nothing blacker than the horror of the cross. And yet God meant it for the ultimate good. John talks about the Lamb slain from the creation of the world. The cross was not God's plan B or Z. It was his means all along to rescue not just humanity but the whole creation. It's in the horror of that, that the unholy trinity (the dragon and the two beasts as described in Revelation 13) is defeated, without humanity being wiped out. The cross of the Lamb defeats the number of the Beast.

CONSIDER: In the words of Bob Dylan, 'You gotta serve somebody. It may be the devil, or it may be the Lord, but you gotta serve somebody.' Your name is either in the Lamb's book of life, or you have the mark of the beast. Which one do you choose? Do you have the mark of the Lamb, or the number of the Beast?

RECOMMENDED FURTHER READING:
Blessed – Nancy Guthrie

PRAYER: O Lord, we praise your Name that you have defeated death and the devil. We thank you that though Satan, the Beast, seeks to place his mark upon all humanity, yet you are rescuing a number that no one can count, and bringing them into the glorious freedom of your kingdom. O Lord grant that I may be in your Book of Life. Amen.

QUESTION: Is heaven boring?

BIBLE READING: Philippians 1

TEXT: 'For to me, to live is Christ and to die is gain. If I am to go on living in the body, this will mean fruitful labour for me. Yet what shall I choose? I do not know! I am torn between the two: I desire to depart and be with Christ, which is better by far'(Philippians 1:21-23).

There is this really strange idea – that hell is a fun place to be, and heaven is boring. Hell is where you party with all your mates – and heaven is an eternal church service. The devil is the father of lies – and this is one of his biggest ones – and one of the most dangerous. Hell is hell. It is not possible to conceive of a worst place to be. Hell is not just darkness, torture and loneliness. It is also the most boring place you could ever be – the same endless hellish repetition. Heaven is heaven – it is not possible to conceive of a better place. And it is a place of joy, music, life and infinite variety.

We are sometimes so immersed in our culture and its memes that we do not realise how much it affects us. As a young Christian I was walking on the beach in Brora in the Scottish Highlands. I was at a missionary conference where the speaker was a wonderful man called Dick Dowsett. It was midnight and the moon was shining off the water. I turned to Dick and said – 'Mr Dowsett, I have a problem'. 'What is it, David?' 'Well, it's all this. It's so beautiful. I don't want to leave it and go to heaven'. 'Why? What do you imagine heaven is like?' 'I'm not sure, but I think it's a bit like a church service that goes on forever.' He laughed and again asked: 'Where would you like to visit on earth before you go to heaven?' 'I want to go to Beijing, Barcelona, Sydney and many other places.' 'David, you need to understand that Beijing, Barcelona and Sydney will be in heaven – or at least the good that they represent, the beauty they have – without all the bad bits. Everything good on this earth is in heaven – this is just the beginning.'

It was an enormously helpful conversation for me. I began to learn to stop thinking of heaven as some kind of ethereal almost non-physical place. Instead, I came to see heaven as the ultimate reality and this world as what C.S. Lewis calls 'the shadowlands'. In other words, all the joy, beauty and love in this world, is just a taster for the real party. That's why we are told that the invitation to follow Christ, is really an invitation to the greatest wedding party in the universe. 'Blessed are those who are invited to the wedding supper of the Lamb' (Revelation 19:9).

That's why Paul longed to go to heaven – because it meant that he would be with Christ. He knew that he had a job to do on this earth – he knew that Christ was in and with him on this earth. But that was always tempered by sin and its effects – both his own and others. Heaven is a sinless place. And it is the place of ultimate beauty, joy and interest – because Christ is there. You will never get bored – because it won't be about you – it's about Christ. And it is impossible for Christ to be boring.

Even the image of an eternal boring church service is wrong. Yes, there have been times when a church service seems as if it was going on forever and it was more like purgatory than heaven. But I hope you have had, or will have the experience, I have had a few times – where the sense of God's presence, the joy and the beauty was so dominant that the time passed so quickly, it seemed as though heaven had come to earth, and you wished it would go on forever! It will. But not yet ... that was just a taster – wait until you get to the real party!

Another way of putting it is from the final book of the Narnia stories – *The Last Battle*. It is one of my favourite books ever. I don't know how many times I have read it! Each time I read it; it seems as though I have learned something new. For me it has been most helpful about heaven.

At one point Jewel the Unicorn delights: 'I have come home at last! This is my real country! I belong here. This is the land I have been looking for all my life, though I never knew it till now...Come further up, come further in!'

Our experience in this life is one of decay. Change and decay in all around I see. Everything is running down. We have to keep moving, adding, changing in order to stop it decaying. In heaven it is the opposite. Everything is being renewed. There is always something new to learn. A new song to sing. New experiences. It is never ending. And never boring!

CONSIDER: Where would you rather be? In a place of endless boredom, misery and loneliness; or a place of endless variety, joy and company? Jesus came to save us from ourselves. He went to heaven to prepare 'many mansions'. Have you accepted his invitation to join him there? If you are a Christian – why do you long for the temporary, vain and fake jewels of this world, when you have the crown of Christ?!

RECOMMENDED FURTHER READING:
The Last Battle – C.S. Lewis

PRAYER Lord, forgive us that we too easily listen to the lies of the evil one – as if life with you could ever be boring! Help us to get rid of the false images we have of heaven – and enable us on this earth to get a foretaste of what heaven will be like, so that we do long for it and you even more. Lord, take us home. Amen.

BIBLE READING: John 14:1-14

TEXT: Jesus answered, 'I am the way and the truth and the life. No one comes to the father except through me' (John 14:6).

This is a question that I am often asked. At a superficial level to the vast majority of people in the Western world it appears obvious that all religions are just different pathways to the same God, and that to claim otherwise is to show the kind of arrogance that leads to hatred, intolerance and religious wars.

There is a great book by my friend Andy Bannister which answers this important question in more depth and is a great read. In it he cites the Anglican vicar and journalist Giles Fraser

'Christians should remind themselves that Muslims are our brothers and sisters with whom we share a faith in the living God.' And President Joe Biden, a professing Catholic, 'I wish we taught more in our schools about the Islamic faith ... [What people] don't realise is that we all come from the same root here in terms of our fundamental, basic beliefs.'

Well, I wish we were taught more about Islam in our schools. I used to teach religious education in a school in Scotland – amongst other things I taught about Islam. Why? How could I as a Christian minister teach about Islam? Because I think it is important for us to understand the second largest religion in the world. It is not good to be ignorant of such an important worldview. It is possible to teach about something without endorsing it.

I found reading the Qur'an very enlightening – and listening to Muslim apologists like Ahmed Deedat helped me to understand that there is a fundamental difference between the Christian and the Islamic view of God. Once I was involved in a debate with a Muslim friend, when a member of the audience furiously challenged me: 'How dare you say we believe in different Gods?! That is an outrageous and intolerant thing to say.' Before I could respond my Islamic opponent asked to speak. 'I know what I believe, I know what my brother David believes, but I have no idea what you believe!' After the same meeting a woman in a burka came up to me and we had the most fascinating conversation: 'David, do you really believe that there is one God, that he is sovereign, the creator of all things, and that there is a heaven and hell?' 'Yes, absolutely'. 'Well, you are the most unusual Christian I have ever met – you are almost a Muslim. If it were not for Jesus, you would be!' I wanted to respond, 'Thank Allah for Jesus!'

Because that is the fundamental difference. Whilst Christians and Muslims are monotheists – believing that there is one God – who is all powerful, all knowing and present everywhere – we disagree about the nature of God. For Christians God is the Trinity – Father, Son and Holy Spirit. For Muslims that is blasphemous. 'They are unbelievers who say, God is the Messiah, Mary's son ... surely whoever associates anything with God, God shall prohibit him entrance to Paradise and his home shall be the Fire. None shall help the evildoers' (Qur'an 5.73). Jesus is God. You cannot have an almighty God who is Trinity and an almighty God who is not Trinity.

There is however another aspect to the question of whether Islam is a pathway to knowing God. Nowhere in the Qur'an does it say that it is possible to know God. For the Muslim that is impossible. All you can do is have correct beliefs about God. But as Jesus says in John 14:6 there is a way to know the Father – and that is through him. He is not only 'a' way – he is the only way.

Islam will not lead you to the knowledge of God. But because the Qur'an mentions Jesus in ninety verses and names him Isa in twenty-five it may lead someone to seek him in God's Word – the Bible. The Bible teaches that all human beings are made in the image of God, and that he has set the burden of eternity in our hearts. In other words, we have a longing for him. Perhaps it might be that Muslims are seeking Allah – but they will ultimately only find him if they find Jesus.

CONSIDER: Why is it not exclusive to acknowledge Jesus as the only way? If Jesus offers himself as the source of salvation for everyone, then surely that is as inclusive as possible? Consider how you can take the truths within Islam, to lead people to the One who is The Truth.

RECOMMENDED FURTHER READING:

Do Muslims and Christians Worship the Same God? – Andy Bannister
Where to Start with Islam – Samuel Green
See also *ASK 35*

PRAYER: Lord God – how can we know you, the unknowable one, unless you reveal yourself to us? We bless and praise your Name that you are the God who reveals himself, in creation, through the prophets, and in these last days by your Son, who is your express image and exact representation. To know Jesus is to know you. We pray O Lord for our Muslim friends. Reveal yourself to them – that they may know you, and the Christ you have sent, that they may have eternal life, in Jesus Name. Amen.

QUESTION: If God has predestined everything, why bother? Do I have free will?

BIBLE READING: John 15

TEXT: 'You did not choose me, but I chose you and appointed you to go and bear fruit—fruit that will last. Then the Father will give you whatever you ask in my name' (John 15:16).

If being asked about other religions is one of the most common questions asked by non-Christian young people, being asked about 'predestination' is one of the most common I am asked when visiting church youth groups. Sometimes I think the question is asked by those who have a real problem with the doctrine, but I suspect that at other times it is asked by those who like a bit of obtuse theological argument, and want to show how clever they are.

I am assuming that you are not one of the latter. That this really is an important issue for you. At first glance the question is a disturbing one that seems to make sense. After all, if God has predestined everything then surely we are trapped – there is nothing we can do? We do not have free will and the whole preaching of the Gospel and the call to repent and believe is just a game. This view was perhaps best expressed by the Scottish poet Robbie Burns in his poem 'Holy Willie's Prayer'. Here is the English translation of the Scots!

> O Thou, who in the heavens does dwell,
> [And] As it pleases best Thyself,
> Sends one to heaven and ten to hell,
> All for Thy glory,
> And not for any good or bad
> They've done during their lifetime!

Burn's poem is a poem about a religious hypocrite. It reflects a common misunderstanding of predestination and salvation. God does not send people to hell irrespective of what they have done. Rather, the Bible tells us that the dead are judged according to what they have done. (Revelation 20:12). God is just. He does not lie. He does not play games. He is pure justice and pure goodness. Those who go to hell, go there because they have chosen to go there. They have chosen to be without God – which is hell. And God gives them what they have lived for.

But the other side of that coin is that those who go to heaven, go because Christ has chosen them. 'In him we were also chosen, having been predestined according to the plan of him who works out everything in conformity with the purpose of his will' (Ephesians 1:11).

As Jesus told his disciples – you did not choose me, but I chose you. The teaching is clear but there are some obvious questions which arise from it.

Do I have free will? Yes – but it's not absolute. Your will cannot determine anything against your nature. You could will to fly but you will never get off the ground just because you will it – no matter how much you flap your arms! The trouble with our will is, as Martin Luther pointed out in his book *The Bondage of the Will,* that we are bound by our natures. We need a new nature that we may freely choose to enter the kingdom of God. Without being born again of the Spirit, we cannot even see the Kingdom of God, never mind enter it!

Is it fair? Yes. God is not unjust. How can it be unfair if we get what we have chosen? No one goes to hell who has not chosen to go there. No one goes to heaven who has not been chosen.

Am I chosen? The Puritan Thomas Manton answered this question helpfully: 'We know God to be ours by giving ourselves up to be his. His choice and election of us is a secret until it be evidenced by our choice of him, till we choose him for our portion' (Works of Manton Vol. 7, p.447).

Your task is not to work out whether you have been chosen; your task is to believe and repent. When you do so then you will know that you have been chosen. I once heard an old preacher describe it in this way. Before you become a Christian you are standing before a door above which is the motto – 'whosoever will may come'. When you become a Christian and walk through the door, you turn round and see another motto on the other side of the door 'chosen according to the foreknowledge of God' (1 Peter 1:2).

I know that this question is often asked because people find the doctrine of predestination (or election, or the sovereignty of God), to be a disturbing one. But, as John

Calvin, pointed out – it is not meant to be like that. In fact, if it is taught well, it is one of the most comforting teachings you can have. As an eighteen-year-old student in the University of Edinburgh I recall the impact on my life when I discovered that my salvation did not depend ultimately on my choice, but on God's. Rather than being a restricting and depressing doctrine – it freed me and gave me a great assurance and joy. I pray that you will know the same.

CONSIDER: If God has chosen you, the Spirit has given you new birth and the Son given you new life, why would you think it didn't matter what you did? Predestination is not an excuse for not bothering – it is the greatest reason to bother! We care and love because he first loved us!

RECOMMENDED FURTHER READING:
Chosen by God – R.C. Sproul
And this article by John Piper – *https://www.desiringgod.org/ articles/before-you-believed-you-belonged*

PRAYER: 'Oh, the depth of the riches
of the wisdom and knowledge of God!
How unsearchable his judgments,
and his paths beyond tracing out!
'Who has known the mind of the Lord?
Or who has been his counsellor?'
'Who has ever given to God,
that God should repay him?'
For from him and through him and to him are all things.
To him be the glory for ever! Amen (Romans 11:33-36).

29. GOD AND THE DEVILS

BIBLE READING: Acts 4:23-31

TEXT: 'They did what your power and will had decided beforehand should happen' (Acts 4:28).

Sometimes people get a little obsessed by the devil or evil spirits. They see demons everywhere and blame them for everything – like the student who said 'I have a demon of laziness!' 'The devil made me do it' is an excuse as old as the Fall. But other people go to the opposite extreme – they do not believe in the reality of the devil and his demons. 'The greatest trick the devil ever pulled was convincing the world he didn't exist' (Kaiser Sose, in the film *The Usual Suspects*). Both errors are fatal – As C.S. Lewis wrote in *The Screwtape Letters* 'there are two equal and opposite errors into which our race can fall about the devils.

123

One is to disbelieve in their existence. The other is to believe and feel an excessive and unhealthy interest in them.'

Another error is to adopt the belief that God and the devil are equal and opposite powers. The world is divided equally into good and bad, and we have to choose which power we will serve. But although the devil is powerful, he is still a created being whose power is limited. He may be called the ruler of this world, or the prince of Darkness but he is still subject to the King of Kings. And that is where you will find the answer to your question.

The African Christian, Augustine, wrote about how God is so powerful that he can even take evil and bring good out of it. 'And, in the universe, even that which is called evil, when it is regulated and put in its own place, only enhances our admiration of the good; for we enjoy and value the good more when we compare it with the evil. For the Almighty God, who, as even the heathen acknowledge, has supreme power over all things, being Himself supremely good, would never permit the existence of anything evil among His works, if he were not so omnipotent and good that he can bring good even out of evil' (Augustine - Enchiridion ch.11).

Augustine also dealt with the question of God creating evil. He said that evil is not a created thing - it is just the absence of good. When God created the devil as a mighty angel, he was not creating evil - but when the devil chose to turn away from God that is how evil - with all its consequences entered the universe. Ever since then the devil has been the Deceiver seeking to destroy all that God has created good. But God is so powerful he can even turn that destructive force into good.

Take for example the story of King Saul in 1 Samuel: 'The Spirit of the LORD had departed from Saul, and an evil spirit from the LORD tormented him.' (1 Samuel 16:14). Saul was God's anointed king and yet he had disobeyed God and turned away from him. God permitted an evil spirit to torment him – why? One reason is that that was the way that David was introduced into Saul's life. It was only his music that could soothe Saul and help him. Ultimately David was to become king, and Christ was to come from the line of David! Whilst the devils were tormenting, God was working out his plan of salvation.

At the Last Supper, Satan entered Judas (John 13:27). As a result, Judas betrayed Jesus and handed him over to be crucified. Surely this was a great evil and a great victory for Satan. Indeed, it was but it was a false victory. Because as our text says, 'they did what your power and will had decided beforehand should happen'. God was working out his plan of salvation.

There are other examples. In Acts chapter 5 we read of how Satan filled their hearts so that Ananias and Sapphira lied to the Holy Spirit – and both of them died. This filled the whole church with 'great fear' and all those who heard about it. In 1 Corinthians 5 Paul talks about handing a man over to Satan, so that whilst his flesh would be destroyed his spirit would be saved on the day of the Lord. And in 2 Corinthians 12 Paul speaks about how a messenger of Satan was sent to him – and that is how he learned more of the grace and power of God.

The point is not that there is a battle between the devil and Christ where we don't know who the winner is! The point is that Christ is so great that even the attacks of the devil can be used for good. 'And we know that in all things God works for the good of those who love him, who have been called according to his purpose' (Romans 8:28). The greatest question we have to ask is not whether the devil will attack us, but rather whether we love God.

CONSIDER: If the devil is on a chain why should we be afraid? If God can even take evil things and turn them for our ultimate good, why should we be afraid? If the world seems in chaos, but the nations are just like a drop in the bucket to God, why should we be afraid? Fear not!

RECOMMENDED FURTHER READING:
Did the Devil Make Me Do It? – Mike McKinley
Satan Cast Out – Frederick S Leahy

PRAYER: : 'Our Father in heaven,
hallowed be your name,
your kingdom come,
your will be done
on earth as it is in heaven.
Give us today our daily bread.
Forgive us our debts,
as we also have forgiven our debtors.
And lead us not into temptation,
but deliver us from the evil one' (Matthew 6:9–13).

QUESTION: Where do you go when you die? What is it like to be dead?

QUESTION: Where do you go when you die? What is it like to be dead?

BIBLE READING: Luke 23:36-43

TEXT: Jesus answered him, 'Truly I tell you; today you will be with me in paradise' (Luke 23:43).

Recently I read an article in *The Guardian* by the philosopher, Scott Hershovitz in which he answered 'questions that confound children and adults alike'. I found it to be really sad. Although *The Guardian* printed it as something helpful and life fulfilling.

There were two questions in particular where he gave not only a wrong, but also a dangerous answer.

Where do you go when you die? Homer, 7
'It's hard to say for sure, since nobody who is dead can tell us. Some people believe in an afterlife – they think we might go to

heaven if we're lucky. But I think we simply cease to exist – that we aren't anywhere.'

That makes some people sad. The universe will be around for billions or trillions of years after we have gone. We only get to hang out here for a little while. But I think it's amazing that we get to be here at all – to explore the world and have fun. So enjoy it, Homer, and don't worry too much about death.'

What is it like to be dead? Arthur, 8

'Same deal, Arthur. We don't know for sure. But I think the answer is: it's not like anything at all. Before you were born, there was nothing like the experience of being you, since you didn't exist. And the same will be true when you're dead. It won't be like anything, since you won't exist any more. And that's okay – in fact, it's good news. Being dead won't bother you. You won't even know that you're dead.'

His whole message is – don't worry. You are only here for a short time. Just enjoy it. And then you are dead. You will feel nothing. You will remember nothing. Indeed, in the context of the universe you are meaningless. In the words of another philosopher, Bertrand Russell, you are a 'blob of carbon floating from one meaningless existence to another'.

God gives us a very different answer. In a café in Chelmsford, England, I was once asked by a man with a big A (for atheist) on his t-shirt; 'who do you think you are? You are just a speck of dust on a tiny planet in the midst of a vast universe'. To which I replied, 'You are indeed correct, sir. If I accept your philosophy. But if I accept what God says, I am someone made in the image of the Creator of this whole universe, someone whose Son died that I might be in the new heavens and the new earth. In your philosophy I am worthless. In God's I am priceless!'

In the book of Ecclesiastes 3:11 Solomon tells us that 'God has set eternity in the human heart'. This means you and I have a sense of the eternal. Philosophers like Scott try to deny that sense of the eternal – but they are denying what their own soul tells them.

When I was struggling, trying to be an atheist, I tried really hard to imagine not existing. It just didn't work. I couldn't do it. Eternity was set in my heart. I knew that when I died that was not the end.

So, what happens when you die? If you are a Christian, then it is as though you have fallen asleep. Like the thief on the cross in our text you will go immediately to be with Christ in heaven, and on the last day, your body and soul will be reunited, and renewed and you will live in the new heavens and the new earth forever. The billionaire owner of Tesla and Twitter, Elon Musk, tweeted 'I don't want to live forever.' And it's not just the richest man in the world who thinks that. Recently I spoke to some teenagers who had exactly the same thought. But they do that because they are really saying that they don't want to live this life forever. In heaven it's a whole different life, in a wholly renewed world. I don't know what that will be like. I cannot describe it – but I do know that it will be a million times better than the most beautiful thing you have ever experienced on earth. (See number 26 for the question is heaven boring?).

But not everyone goes to heaven. There are those who do not want to be with God – and so he grants them their desire. After the day of judgement, they go to the place that is without God – hell. It is the exact opposite of heaven. A place – not of fun and a good time with your mates – but a place of loneliness, darkness, isolation and pain. AC/DC not only sang about a 'Highway to Hell', they also sang that 'Hell Ain't a Bad Place to Be'. But hell is. There could be no worse place.

When you or I die, we will go to either heaven or hell. Jesus put it very simply to another philosopher/teacher, Nicodemus; 'For God so loved the world that he gave his one and only Son, that whoever believes in him would not perish but have eternal life. For God did not send his Son into the world to condemn the world, but to save the world through him' (John 3:16-17). Why would you refuse him? Why would you choose heaven over hell?

CONSIDER: Are you, like most normal human beings, scared of death? Why? Does the idea of the eternal frighten you? Where would you like to go when you die? Heaven or hell? Why not accept Jesus' offer of eternal life?

RECOMMENDED FURTHER READING:
What Happens When I Die? – Marcus Nodder
What Happens When We Die? – Chris Morphew

PRAYER: O Lord Jesus, this is such a serious, strange and solemn subject. Sometimes it hurts us to think about it. Help us to look to you. Give us understanding. Save us from hell, deliver us from death and bring us to live with you forever. Amen.

31 BEFORE BIRTH

BIBLE READING: Jeremiah 1

TEXT: 'Before I formed you in the womb I knew you, before you were born, I set you apart; I appointed you as a prophet to the nations' (Jeremiah 1:5).

Do we exist before we are born? It's a more complex question than you might think!

Let's return to the philosopher we mentioned in the last chapter – Scott Hershovitz. He was asked by a girl called Melia: 'Where was I before I was born and before I was in your belly?' 'Melia, bad news: you were never in my belly. But you have good company in wondering where you were before you were born ...'

Then he was asked by a boy called Josh – 'Where was I before I was here?'

'Nowhere! The universe has been around for billions of years, but you weren't part of it until very recently. I wasn't either, though I've been here a bit longer than you.

Have you ever made something new - like a picture? It wasn't anywhere until you made it. And you're just the same. You weren't anywhere until your parents made you.'

This is the worldview of atheistic naturalism. You were nowhere, and you are going nowhere. You're on the road to annihilation. And therefore, ultimately in the grand scheme of things you are meaningless. Read the book of Ecclesiastes to see what that feels like. 'Surely the fate of human beings is like that of animals; the same fate awaits them both. As one dies, so does the other. All have the same breath; humans have no advantage over animals. Everything is meaningless' (Ecclesiastes 3:19).

But what does the Bible have to say about our existence before we were born. Where were you before you were born? You were in your mother's womb. You existed then. 'For you created my inmost being; you knit me together in my mother's womb' (Psalm 139:13). This is important because there are people today who say that a person does not come into existence until they are actually born. That is not what either the Bible or science teaches. When you were in the womb, you were not a blob, or a lifeless group of cells. You were you.

But what about before then? Some religions argue that you existed in a previous life. They believe in reincarnation - the idea that you existed before and are 'reborn' into your current body. I have occasionally met people who think that they were an Egyptian Pharaoh or a Greek princess in a previous life. It's surprising that they never think they were a cockroach! But reincarnation is just another confusing lie from the Father of Lies. As the Scottish band, the Proclaimers put it in their song 'The More I Believe':

'I don't believe in reincarnation
I'm not coming back as a flower
I don't bow my head to kings or priests
'Cause I believe in your higher power.'

There is one person who existed before he was in his mother's womb. That is Jesus. 'In the beginning was the Word, and the Word was with God, and the Word was God' (John 1:1). This Word became flesh and dwelt among us. Jesus is eternal. You are not. Jesus did not have a beginning, you did. Isn't it amazing that the One who created everything was himself created as a human in the womb of Mary?!

So, the answer to the question where were you before you were conceived in your mother's womb - is that you did not exist. Unlike Jesus you are not eternal - with no beginning. But that is not the end of the story. Look at our verse from Jeremiah. 'Before I formed you in the womb, I knew you'. God who is outside, as well as inside, time and space - knew about Jeremiah - and he knows about you. In other words, you are not a random accident in a meaningless world. All the days ordained for you were written in God's book before one of them came to be (Psalm 139:16).

All of this is so incredible, wonderful, and beautiful. But I don't want to finish there.

Although we don't believe in reincarnation, we do believe in the new birth. When Jesus told Nicodemus that if he wanted to see the kingdom of God he would have to be born again, he replied, 'How can someone be born when they are old? Surely, they cannot enter a second time into their mother's womb to be born?' (John 3:4). Nicodemus was of course right. But Jesus was not talking about another physical birth. He was talking about spiritual birth – or to be more accurate birth by the Holy Spirit. Your temporary life on earth is dependent on your being born. Your eternal life in heaven is dependent on your being born again!

CONSIDER: It is good for us to think about who we are and where we come from. Who are your ancestors? What is our heritage? It is good to celebrate the day of our birth. But is it not even more important to think about where we are going? And how we get there? Is not the day of our second birth even more important than our first?

RECOMMENDED FURTHER READING:
Who am I? – Jerry Bridges.

PRAYER: How precious to me are your thoughts, God! How vast is the sum of them! Search me, God, and know my heart; test me and know my anxious thought. See if there is any offensive way in me, and lead me in the way everlasting. Amen (Psalm 139:17, 23-24).

32. THE SECOND COMING

QUESTION: When will Jesus come back? Also, who is Jesus going to take and who is he going to leave behind? Will Jesus also take the innocent children of the people who are not Christians?

BIBLE READING: Matthew 24:36-51

TEXT: 'So you also must be ready, because the Son of Man will come at an hour you do not expect him' (Matthew 24:44).

Mel Gibson's *The Passion of the Christ* was one of the biggest grossing films ever. As is the case with successful movies there has to be a part two. So what follows the Cross? At the time of writing Gibson is planning *The Passion of the Christ: Resurrection* which, according to the trailers will have as much to do with the Second Coming of Christ – as it will with the actual resurrection. Given the speculation about the Second Coming, and the drama involved, it certainly offers a filmmaker like Gibson a great opportunity for special effects and bloodthirsty horror. And therein lies the problem. There has been far too much speculation about the Second Coming. It is good for us to avoid both the speculation that adds to the Bible, or the unbelief that takes away from it.

In *ASK* question 23 was about the end of the world – I won't repeat what is said there – other than to remind you that we don't know when the end of the world will be. And so, we don't know when the return of Jesus will be – although we can be sure that every day brings it a day closer.

But let's look at Matthew 24 and draw from it some certainties about the second coming which I hope will help answer your questions.

It will happen. The Second Coming refers to the visible return of Christ to the earth.

Before it does happen there will be great trouble on the earth, great apostasy in the Church, and many false messiahs.

The Second Coming, unlike the First, will be with great power and glory (v. 30). Everyone will see. This will be a world -wide event – and will signal the end of the world.

We do not know when it will happen. Even Jesus when he was on earth did not know (v. 36).

We need to be ready. Because we do not know when he will come, we must live every day as though he were about to return. It's a bit like your parents going away and leaving you to have the house to yourself. You know they are going to return, and you know they don't want to see the house in a mess. You don't want to upset them, so because you don't know when they are going to come back, you have things ready for them. We are to keep watch.

We are to long for it. At least Christians are. Again, it's like a child standing at the window waiting for their father to return. Or have you ever seen one of those welcome home videos of soldiers returning from a tour of duty overseas? The child longs to see their parent, or their returned father. So, we must be longing for Jesus. That's why the early Christians prayed 'Maranatha' (1 Corinthians 16:22). Maranatha is one of the few words in the Bible that is in Aramaic – the language that Jesus spoke. Maranatha means 'Come, O Lord'. It is also reflected in the Greek of the second last verse of the Bible (Revelation 22:20) – 'Amen, Come, Lord Jesus'.

You ask about who Jesus will leave behind. I suspect that is because you have been influenced by a particular teaching about the Second Coming, called the Rapture. This is the belief that Jesus will return secretly in the clouds and 'rapture' his people up to heaven, then he will return again with his people to reign for a thousand years, then he will go away, and then return again. I'm not sure how many 'comings' that makes! It seems to me far more complex than the Bible is. I think the biblical evidence is that there will only be one Second Coming – and that that will usher in the end of the world, the judgement day, the second resurrection (that is the reuniting of believers' spirits with their bodies). It will be an astonishing event. No one will be 'left behind' – in the sense of being left to live on earth. But only believers in Christ will be gathered with him to take part in the great wedding feast of the Lamb.

'After that, we who are alive and are left will be caught up together with them in the clouds to meet the Lord in the air. And so we will be with the Lord forever' (1 Thessalonians 4:17.)

In terms of your question about children, go back to question 16 where we discuss that.

The important thing for you and I is that we do not get so caught up in the speculation about details that we forget the most important truth here – Jesus is returning, and we need to be ready for that.

CONSIDER: If we really believed that Christ could return at any time, what difference do you think it would, or should, make to our lives? Is this a comforting or challenging truth? Or both?

RECOMMENDED FURTHER READING:
The Momentous Event – W.J. Grier

PRAYER: Lord, we thank you that you have promised to return and that it will be soon. Even so we pray, 'Amen, Come, Lord Jesus.'

BIBLE READING: Exodus 35:30 – 36:1

TEXT: 'He has filled them with skill to do all kinds of work as engravers, designers, embroiderers in blue, purple and scarlet yarn and fine linen, and weavers – all of them skilled workers and designers' (Exodus 35:35).

I used to hate going to art galleries. As a child I thought they were really boring – I wanted to go to a play park or a football game – anything other than an art gallery. But times change. Now, the first thing I do when I head to a city is look for its art gallery. For some people art galleries are like cathedrals – they are the nearest they get to a transcendent experience.

And that for some Christians is the problem. They think that art is idolatry – that art replaces God for some people. Christians are 'spiritual' people and should have nothing to do with the vulgar arts. Some invoke the 2nd commandment, 'you shall not make for yourself an image in the form of anything in heaven above or on the earth beneath or in the waters below' (Exodus 20:4). But they forget the next verse 'you shall not bow down to them or worship them'. The 2nd commandment is not against art - it is against idolatry - the making of images of God.

Solomon knew the ten commandments - yet 'He adorned the temple with precious stones' (2 Chronicles 3:6) because he wanted the temple to be beautiful, for the glory of God. There is such a thing as good art - beautiful art. But there is also the bad.

One art gallery that is a real pleasure to go to is the Metropolitan Museum of Art in New York. The last time I visited the galleries were done chronologically, according to centuries. It was fascinating that every century gallery was absolutely packed with visitors - except the twentieth - where we could have had a game of five a side football! I wondered why? Could it be something to do with the fact that the dominant subject in all the previous centuries was religion and the search for meaning - whereas the 20th century gallery was like a painting of Solomon's words 'Meaningless, meaningless ... everything is meaningless' (Ecclesiastes 1:2)?

This is not to say that a Christian view of art means that the artist should only ever paint religious images - that would be a shallow, cheap and ultimately God-denying view of art. But a Christian view of art works on the premise that we do art because God is the great artist - providing variety, form and infinite colour in his creation. As creative creatures we reflect the Creator. Our text in Exodus talks about God filling the engravers, designers, embroiders and weavers with great skill.

The trouble with so much art today is that it is meaningless and destructive. I am a member of the National Gallery of New

South Wales – and love going to visit it, especially after being in the Botanic Gardens where I get to see the Creator's art close up! I love the European masterpieces and the Aboriginal art. But sometimes there are items that make you wonder – why?! One such was a black canvas with the inscription beside it telling us that the artist had painted a picture and had then just painted over it with black so we would just have to guess what was underneath. Apparently, the gallery paid a six-figure sum for this work of genius! There was another time when I visited a contemporary art gallery where the main display was a can of baked beans in the midst of the floor. This is a classic example of the emperor having no clothes principle! Remember the story of how a fraudster tailor convinced people that the emperor was really wearing an invisible grand set of clothes which only the intelligent could see. If you wanted to appear intelligent, you said that you saw them. It's a bit like that with some modern art. People talk about how insightful and deep it is – until a child comes along and points out it's nothing!

It is not only the meaninglessness and emptiness of some modern art which makes it bad – but also the crass commercialisation. I visited an art gallery in Edinburgh to see some paintings by an artist friend of mine, Robert, who is also a Christian. His paintings are stunning – visit his website to see – https://www.robertmacmillan.co.uk/ One of his large paintings was for sale for £5,000 – but beside it was a work by another artist which was banal and ugly – yet it was for sale for £50,000. I asked the gallery owner which one he would prefer. He had no doubt – Robert's was by far the better painting. So why the price difference? Because of the 'name' of the artist. Basically, Japanese art speculators would come in and buy this painting – not because they liked it – but because they saw it as a financial investment for the future.

The Christian view of art is to see the value of the art not in how much people will pay for it, but rather in how much it reflects the values and beauty of the Creator. That is good art – done with humility, skill, and without pretentiousness. As Francis Schaeffer argues in his wonderful little book on 'Art and the Bible' 'A Christian should use these arts to the glory of God, not just as tracts mind you, but as things of beauty to the glory of God' (Schaeffer p. 18). Sometimes the Christian Church has overreacted against the bad use of art by becoming almost anti-artistic. I much prefer the attitude of churches such as the Dutch Reformed who encouraged art in many different forms.... just look at the paintings of Rembrandt, Vermeer, Jans Hals, Van Steen and many others. This is good art to the glory of God.

CONSIDER: Is good or bad art just a matter of personal taste? Non-Christians can do great art, and Christians can do bad art. But how should our Christianity affect our view of art? Can art be used to point people to the ultimate Artist?

RECOMMENDED FURTHER READING:

Art and the Bible – Francis A. Schaeffer
Modern Art and the Death of a Culture – Hans Rookmaaker

PRAYER: O Lord God, you are the God of great beauty and creativity. You have made us in your image. You have given us the gifts of the arts. May we use whatever gifts you have given us for your glory. Let the beauty of the Lord our God be upon us, and may that beauty be reflected in what we do. In Jesus Name and for his glory. Amen.

QUESTION: Is music spiritual? Is it wrong for a Christian to be a D.J.?

BIBLE READING: Psalm 150

TEXT: 'Let everything that has breath praise the Lord. Praise the Lord' (Psalm 150:6).

Music is so important to human beings. It is such a key part of our lives. At least it is for most of us. This should not surprise us – we are made in the image of God and our God is a singing God. 'The LORD your God is with you, the Mighty Warrior who saves. He will take great delight in you; in his love he will no longer rebuke you but will rejoice over you with singing' (Zephaniah 3:17).

He wants his people to sing praise to him – just read through the book of Psalms! I love the detail recorded in 1 Chronicles 23:5: 'Four thousand are to praise the LORD with

143

the musical instruments I have provided for that purpose.'
Four thousand musicians in the temple of the Lord.

Yes, music is spiritual. Or, using spiritual in the sense of
the Holy Spirit, it can be spiritual. But sometimes it can also
be earthly and destructive. John Calvin in his preface to the
Genevan Psalter wrote this: 'Now among the other things
which are proper for recreating man and giving him pleasure,
music is either the first, or one of the principals; and it is
necessary for us to think that it is a gift of God deputed for
that use. Moreover, because of this, we ought to be the more
careful not to abuse it, for fear of soiling and contaminating it,
converting [it to] our condemnation, where it was dedicated to
our profit and use ... and in fact, we find by experience that it
has a sacred and almost incredible power to move hearts in one
way or another ...'

Music can be very powerful for good or evil. In question 29
we mentioned the positive and soothing impact that the music
of David on the harp had on King Saul. I find myself listening
to some music and marvelling at how beautiful and spiritual
it is. As we saw in the previous chapter on art – music too can
reflect the beauty and creativity of our Creator – our singing
God.

Einstein, as well as being one of the greatest scientists who
has ever lived, was also a musician. He wrote about Mozart
– 'Mozart's music is so pure and beautiful that I see it as a
reflection of the inner beauty of the universe' (McGrath –
A Theory of Everything – p. 101).

Another aspect of music that is reflective of the Creator – is
how diverse and varied it is. Sometimes, when I am asked what
my favourite music is, I'm not sure what to say. I love classical,

folk, rock, jazz and many other forms. Sometimes, like art, our feelings about music can be really subjective, but also like art – there is good and bad music. If you play notes out of key, or sing out of tune, that does not make for good music.

My friend Archie and I spent part of a summer hitchhiking round the Scottish Highlands, staying at youth hostels. Archie had a guitar, and I had a bodhran (an Irish hand drum). Each night we would start a 'ceilidh' (a musical get-together) at the hostel we were staying in. It was great fun for a couple of amateurs - but I will never forget the night an Australian folk singer congratulated us on our harmonies. Harmonies? What harmonies? I was just singing out of tune – still at least he liked it!

However, music can also be good or bad in terms of the purpose for which it is used. Which brings us on to the second part of your question. Is it good for a Christian to be a D.J.? I guess the answer to that depends on what kind of D.J. and in what circumstances. There is a world of difference between playing the tunes at a wedding dance - and being the D.J. down your local night club.

Speaking to some young men in Dundee, I asked them why they went to dance/night clubs. They all stated that it was because they saw them kind of like a meat market (their words) – where they went along and found it very easy to get girls. They told me that because of the highly charged atmosphere, the drugs and the alcohol, it was easy to 'hook up'. I cannot understand how any Christian would want to be part of that – or facilitate that. Walking along City Wharf in the Darling Harbour centre of Sydney I was greatly saddened to see the queues of young people outside the numerous nightclubs. I observed these 'seekers of pleasure' behaving in ways that degraded and demeaned them. As a D.J. in such a club you would be facilitating that. Why?

The bottom line is that music is a gift from God – to be used for his glory and not for our own, or other people's sins. It is spiritual, but we need to make sure that that means not evil spirits, but rather the Holy Spirit. We either sing in harmony with him – or we dance with the devil.

CONSIDER: Can you think of other ways that music can be used for good or bad? Think about the music you listen to. Is it helpful, good, beautiful? Does it help you glorify God? Can you give thanks to God for it?

RECOMMENDED FURTHER READING:
Come let us Sing – Rob Smith (this is a great book on why we sing as Christians).

PRAYER: Lord, we exist to praise you. Let everything that has breath praise the Lord. Help us to glorify you through the gift of music. May the music we listen to, the music we play, and the music we use in church, bring glory to you. May we sing in harmony with you, Amen.

35. MATHS

QUESTION: What is the point of Algebra?

BIBLE READING: Colossians 1:15-20

TEXT: 'He is before all things and in him all things hold together' (Colossians 1:17).

Before we answer the question, it is necessary for us to ask, 'what is algebra'? At school I can remember being taught arithmetic, geometry and algebra under the general heading of mathematics. The dictionary definition of algebra is 'the part of mathematics in which letters and other general systems are used to represent numbers and quantities in formulae and equations'. Mathematics in general, and algebra in particular are essential for science and for much of modern society. As a theologian and historian, I don't personally have much use for them directly – but I do benefit from their fruits – as do you.

Professor John Lennox was the first to convince me of the importance of mathematics, arguing that it was essential to

understanding almost anything! Of course, given that he is
a professor of mathematics at the University of Oxford, you
might think that it is hardly surprising that he would argue
this. But he has more than a point.

Wayne Westenberg argues that 'Mathematics has been and
remains a foundational block in the liberal arts. Throughout
history, the mastery of mathematics has helped us understand
both the creation and the Creator. Such understanding is
far more than mere knowledge. That is the greatest reason
for the study of this discipline.' https://godandmath.files.
wordpress.com/2011/10/westenberg-why-mathematics-and
-christianity.pdf

Perhaps it is easy to understand why maths is so essential
in science – but what does it have to do with God? Surely
mathematics is neutral? 2 + 2 = 4, no matter what faith, or lack
of faith you may have.

Some go even further than that. They argue that maths
actually points us away from God – because they say that
we believe in a 'God of the gaps.' In other words when we
don't understand something we just say that 'God did it'. As
mathematics helps us understand our universe better, then
there is less and less room for God. But as Lennox argues
'When Sir Isaac Newtown discovered the universal law of
gravitation he did not say, 'I have discovered a mechanism
that accounts for planetary motion, therefore there is no agent
God who designed it.' Quite the opposite: precisely because
he understood how it worked, he was moved to increased
admiration for the God who had designed it that way.'

In its immediate application mathematics is neutral and can
be done by anyone. But in its speaking to us as a language we

can only hear if we open our ears and minds and understand Johannes Kepler's point 'The chief aim of all investigations of the external world should be to discover the rational order and harmony which has been imposed on it by God and which He revealed to us in the language of mathematics.'

What is the point of mathematics? It shows us the order and beauty of the created universe, and therefore because that universe is a reflection of the Creator, it shows us the order and beauty of God.

It may seem strange to our modern Western 'logical' minds, but mathematics speaks to us as much of the beauty of God as do music and art.

But let me reverse that a little. Not only does mathematics show us the beauty of God, but God shows us the purpose of mathematics. Just like humanity – it exists to glorify and enjoy him! Augustine's great argument applies to mathematics 'We don't rightly understand anything until we understand its connection with Jesus Christ'.

If you go to the passage, we read in Colossians chapter one you will see that Christ is not only the creator of all things – but that in him all things hold together. The laws of maths are his laws. He is the Logos (John 1:1). He is the one who sustains, preserves and keeps all things in order. The Universe exists because of him. And it continues because of him. And he uses mathematics to do that.

'Every time you solve a math problem, you're relying on the underlying consistency present in math. Any time you see that math still operates consistently, it's testifying that God is still on His throne, faithfully holding all things together.' – Katherine Loop

I'll bet you never thought that all those boring equations could be so important! If, unlike me, you have a gift for mathematics, use it for the glory of God, and for the good of your fellow human beings. Mathematicians are important - like artists, musicians, farmers, healers, carers and writers, they reflect the beauty of the One in whose image they are created.

CONSIDER: What would the world be like if there were no mathematics? What would it be like if there were no mathematicians? How can you use your study of maths to build up your faith, bear witness to Christ and live for the glory of God?

RECOMMENDED FURTHER READING:
Principles of Mathematics Book 1 - Katherine Loop
https://godandmath.com/how-is-math-done-christianly/

PRAYER: Lord Jesus, we thank and praise you that you have the whole world in your hands. In you all things were created. All things have been created through you and for you. You are before all things, and in you all things hold together. We praise you that we can see that in the laws you use to govern the world. Give us understanding, and grant that we may live for your glory. Amen.

BIBLE READING: Luke 7:28-35

TEXT: 'The Son of Man came eating and drinking, and you say, "Here is a glutton and a drunkard, a friend of tax collectors and sinners"' (Luke 7:34).

This is yet another great question. Like many other great questions, it is not as simple as we like to think. On the one hand there are those who cite verses such as Proverbs 13:20 – 'Walk with the wise and become wise, for a companion of fools suffers harm'. On the other there are those who cite the verse above. In fact, the Bible has a lot to say about friends, because friendship is so important to us as human beings.

Let's begin by asking 'what is a friend'? I like the definition in the Encyclopaedia Britannica – 'a state of enduring affection, esteem, intimacy, and trust between two people. In all cultures, friendships are important relationships throughout a person's life span.'

God has made us as social beings. We all need friends. But like all the good things that God has given us the gift of friendship can be misused. We can be so desperate for friends that we end up doing things that we know are wrong. Which is why Paul warns us, 'Do not be misled: "Bad company corrupts good character."' (1 Corinthians 15:33). James reminds us of the consequences of friendship with the world, 'You adulterous people, don't you know that friendship with the world means enmity against God? Therefore, anyone who chooses to be a friend of the world becomes an enemy of God.' (James 4:4) It is possible to be friends with 'worldly' people, but if our friendships lead us away from God then they are not helpful.

This does not mean that we should have no friends who are 'worldly'. If that were the case, we would have to leave the world. But it does mean that we should follow the advice of Proverbs 12:26 'The righteous choose their friends carefully, but the way of the wicked leads them astray.'

When I became a Christian most of my friends were not. What intrigued me was that some were happy for me to be a Christian and did not let it affect our friendship, but others didn't really want to know me now that I had 'become a Bible basher'. Friends who make your friendship conditional upon you thinking and behaving just like them are not really the sort of friends you want.

Jesus was a 'friend of sinners' not because he 'hung out' with people and affirmed or ignored their sin. No – he was a true friend because he wanted to see those people be forgiven and come to really know him. In fact, he wanted to be their friend. If you follow him then you will desire the same.

'One who has unreliable friends soon comes to ruin, but there is a friend who sticks closer than a brother' (Proverbs 18:24). All of our friends will let us down (including our Christian ones), but there is one who never will. If I am truly your friend, then I want to share with you the greatest things I have. What is greater than Christ? He is the friend who sticks closer than a brother.

This is not to say that you are always to be evangelising your friends or suggesting that you will not be their friend unless they become Christians. But it is to say that your love for them means that you want the best for them. Therefore, when you are with your friends you won't want to do anything that points them away from Christ.

That has great practical implications. In the first week of the first term of my first year at Edinburgh University it was a tradition of the hall I stayed in that we all went on a pub crawl – where most got drunk. I didn't want to go, but neither did I want to be seen as a snob or someone who was not prepared to get involved with other people. So, I joined the pub crawl. However, after the first pub I said that I was just going to stay there and play pool. Much to my astonishment many of the others decided they would stay too. They also did not want to join in the drunkenness. You can be friends with people and not be a self-righteous prig!

However, it may be that you will lose some friends because you choose to follow Jesus Christ. But although you may lose them – you have gained him. 'My command is this: Love each other as I have loved you. Greater love has no one than this: to lay down one's life for one's friends' (John 15:12-13). You now have the Son of God as your friend! What a friend we have in Jesus!

CONSIDER: Do you consider your Facebook friends to be real friends? What is a real friend? How many real friends do you have? How can you cultivate real friendship? Why is 'hanging out' not enough? Does being the friend of Jesus make a difference to how you view friendships?

RECOMMENDED FURTHER READING:
Beautifully Distinct – Conversations with Friends on Faith, Life and Culture – Ed. Trillia Newbell
The Four Loves – C.S. Lewis
https://www.thegospelcoalition.org/blogs/kevin-deyoung/jesus-friend-of-sinners-but-how/

PRAYER: Lord Jesus, we thank you for the gift of friendship. May we truly be those who love and serve our friends. When we have been hurt and wounded by them help us to see whether that is good and to forgive when it is bad. Most of all may we rely on you as the greatest friend of all. In your name. Amen.

37. KNOWING GOD

QUESTION: What is God?

BIBLE READING: Isaiah 40

TEXT: 'Do you not know? Have you not heard? The Lord is the everlasting God, the Creator of the ends of the earth. He will not grow tired or weary, and his understanding no one can fathom' (Isaiah 40:28).

This is the ultimate question – although perhaps it would be better to ask, 'who is God?'. There is so much that could be said. In *ASK* we looked at the uncreated God (Question 10), the gender of God (Question 11), the Trinity (Question 12) and the mind of God (Question 13). In fact, most of the questions in *ASK* and in this book are answered on the basis of the character of God, who he is, what he has done, and what he says. But when we talk about God, what are we saying? What do we mean?

Sometimes when people say, 'I don't believe in God' I ask them to tell me about this God that they don't believe in.

155

Invariably they give an answer which prompts the response – 'I don't believe in that God either – now let me tell you about the one that I do'. This is not a question of my God versus theirs – it is a question of reality – of who God really is – not just what we perceive him to be. By definition a god of our own imagination is not God.

One of the best answers to the question 'What (who) is God?' is in the Shorter Catechism (can I suggest you get *The Illustrated Westminster Shorter Catechism* published by Christian Focus – it is a beautiful edition of a really helpful book). Here is question four.

Q: What is God?
A: God is a Spirit, infinite, eternal, and unchangeable, in his being, wisdom, power, holiness, justice, goodness, and truth.

That's a great summary.

We would not know God unless he revealed himself to us. He does. Firstly, we can learn of God's eternal power and divine nature from what he has made (Romans 1:18 -20). All human beings have that knowledge. We also have the awareness of God, and his laws within us (Romans 2:15). But because of our corrupt nature we have lost the knowledge of God. We suppress the truth and even become foolish enough to deny God. So we need God to reveal himself to us. He does so through his Word.

Take, for example, Isaiah chapter 40. As you read through it jot down how many things you learn about God. He is the God who speaks; whose Word endures forever; he is sovereign; he cares for his people; he is greater than all creation because he is the author of all creation; he cannot be understood, nor can we instruct him; the nations and powers of this world are a drop in the bucket compared with him; he cannot be represented through anything we make; he brings the rulers of this world to nothing; he controls the stars; he is the everlasting God, the Creator of the ends of the earth; he never grows tired or weary but he gives strength to the tired and weary.

We can use lots of big words to describe all this. God is omnipresent (he is everywhere); God is omnipotent (he is all powerful); and God is omniscient (he knows everything). I prefer the pictures and images given us in chapters like Isaiah 40.

The point is that we don't make a 'god' in our own image. And we do not sit in judgement upon God. We accept what he says to us about himself, and we humbly seek to know him.

Hebrews chapter 1 tells us that in the past God revealed himself in different ways (prophets, dreams, miracles) but that in these last days the ultimate revelation of God is Jesus. He is 'the radiance of God's glory and the exact representation of his being' (Hebrews 1:3). To know Jesus is to know God. Which is a wonderful thing for us personally. I find God to be incomprehensible – which is as it should be – how could a finite and limited mind like mine expect to comprehend and understand the Infinite? But I love the idea that when I look at Jesus (as he is given to us in his Word) I see exactly what God is like. The ultimate answer to your question is just simply – look at Jesus. God is like Jesus. God is Jesus.

There is one aspect of God that I think is missing from the Shorter Catechism answer. That is found in 1 John 4:16 where the statement is made, 'God is love'. It is a profound and deep statement which means a lot more than the shallow cultural meme 'love is love'. To know that God is love, to know that he so loved the world that he gave his only Son (John 3:16), to know that we are to walk in love – is to have the deepest knowledge of the greatest truth. I pray that you would know this personal, almighty, all knowing, all powerful, all loving God.

CONSIDER: If God is incomprehensible, how can we possibly know him? Only if he reveals himself to us. How does he do that? Do you accept the revelation of God in Jesus Christ? Is this a real question to you, or just a matter for argument?

RECOMMENDED FURTHER READING:
Knowing God – J.I. Packer

PRAYER: O Lord God, how can I know you? To know you is to have eternal life – and yet we have been shut out from the tree of life. Reveal yourself to me. Have mercy upon me. Let me know your love, your truth, your faithfulness, your mercy. Lord, I want to see Jesus. Open the eyes of my heart, forgive me and grant me eternal life, for your glory. Amen.

38: EVIDENCE AGAINST GOD

BIBLE READING: Psalm 14

TEXT: 'The fool says in his heart, there is no God. They are corrupt, their deeds are vile; there is no one who does good' (Psalm 14:1).

What is the evidence for God? When asked that question I can cite lots of things – Creation, the human mind and spirit, the moral law, beauty, religion, experience, history, the Church, the Bible and Jesus (*The Dawkins Letters* pp. 154-157). In terms of Jesus, I tried to give the evidence for him in *Magnificent Obsession*. I have spent a lot of my life trying to provide the evidence for God. But what if it was the other way round? Your question is one I have been asked many times – what if you were given evidence to show that God isn't real – would you continue in your faith?

The answer to that is simply no – I could not continue. Like the late great atheist Anthony Flew I follow the maxim, I go where the evidence leads me. (Flew eventually became a believer in God – if not Christ – precisely because of the evidence. See his book – *There is a God*.) If someone showed me, for example, the bones of Jesus, then my faith is over – because my faith is in the risen Christ. However, that is not the same as saying that if someone showed me that something I believed was wrong, that I would then give up the whole Christian faith. On secondary issues I might have to reassess aspects of my belief, but I would not give up faith in Jesus Christ – because my faith in Christ does not depend on me being right about every jot and tittle.

But what evidence could there be for God not existing? I don't think that question even makes sense. It's like asking if someone showed evidence that your wife did not exist would you still be married to her?! Now it is theoretically possible that someone could outargue me, drug me and convince me that my wife was really a figment of my imagination, and that I was just dreaming her – but then you have moved away from the realms of rational argument to a kind of surreal Matrix movie fantasy.

But you may think that whilst the existence of my wife is not in doubt, the evidence for God is not nearly as strong. Perhaps in my own experience that might be the case – but when everything is taken together, I would suggest that the evidence for God is more convincing and persuasive than the evidence for the existence of your nearest and dearest.

Do I ever doubt that? Yes – I have had my periods of doubts – what the puritan John Flavel calls 'atheistic thoughts'. I can remember three periods of real spiritual darkness. The first was when, not long after becoming a Christian, I read Marxist historian Christopher Hill's *The World Turned Upside Down*. In it he argued that the English puritans engaged in one of the most successful brainwashing exercises in history. The thought struck me – 'what if I have been brainwashed?' Many Christians who have been brought up in Christian homes often go through the same experience – as the devil seeks to deceive them out of their faith.

How did I get through that experience? The black holes of atheism are normally based upon feelings and spiritual attacks – not upon rational thought or evidence. I looked at the evidence and I came down to the foundations and asked, what do I believe? At that stage there were many things I doubted but the one thin sliver of faith I had left was that I believed in Jesus Christ and that he had died for my sins and was now alive. It was enough.

The other two experiences were very similar – although they were even more dependent on feelings rather than rational reasons. It's a bit like the kind of irrational feeling someone has when they are standing on top of some high cliffs and begin to wonder what it would be like to jump. To obey that instinct would be suicide. To listen to our doubts and fears and jump into the black hole of atheism is spiritual suicide.

In summary, it is foolish to go against the overwhelming evidence for the God of the Bible. He has provided us with so much evidence that the only way we cannot see it is to deliberately shut our eyes and claim it doesn't exist. That is why the Bible calls it foolish. In today's world there are people who believe in wacky conspiracy theories – and it is impossible to argue them out of it. Why? Because everything you say is part of the conspiracy. In the same way the person who says in his heart that there is no God is a fool. They won't be persuaded by rational argument or evidence, because they didn't come to disbelieve because of rational argument or evidence.

The question for you is not really whether there is a God – but whether you trust him and follow him. The real question is what do you think of Jesus Christ?

CONSIDER: Do you think that we are able to sit in judgement upon God? Are our minds big enough, honest enough, and clear enough to be able to make those pronouncements? Do you agree that the temptation to atheism comes more from feelings and spiritual attacks, than it does from evidence? How do you think you can combat these?

RECOMMENDED FURTHER READING:
The Dawkins Letters – David Robertson

PRAYER: O Lord, you look down from heaven to see if there are any who understand, who seek you. We thank you that you are present in the midst of your people – and we pray that we would be faithful and continue to worship. When we walk in darkness, O Lord, grant us light. When we are full of fear, give us faith. When we doubt, help us to delight in you, in Jesus Name. Amen.

Question: To what extent does God forgive?

BIBLE READING: Luke 23:26-43

TEXT: Jesus said, 'Father, forgive them, for they do not know what they are doing' (Luke 23:34).

To know that you are forgiven is one of the greatest things, perhaps the greatest thing you can know. Imagine that you are in great debt – you owe a lot of money. You are worried about how you can pay it off. You fear that you will lose your home, your friends, perhaps even your liberty. You are then taken to court, only to discover that someone has paid every penny that you owe. You are forgiven, you are free.

Jesus taught us to pray – 'And forgive us out debts, as we also have forgiven our debtors' (Matthew 6:12). Sin is a debt against God. But who can pay that debt? Not you. Not the Church. Not any religion. Only Christ.

In *ASK* question 17 we looked at how we get forgiveness – and how costly it really is. Forgiveness is not cheap. In fact, the debt we owed is so great that only the blood of the Son of God can pay it.

Why is sin so hard to forgive? Because it is against a pure and holy God – who cannot allow anything evil to spoil his creation or diminish his Glory. His eyes are too pure to even look upon evil and he cannot tolerate wrongdoing (Habakkuk 1:13). God must be faithful to his own standards; he must remain righteous. Yet he loves us and wants to bring peace. How can 'love and faithfulness meet together'? (Psalm 85:10). How can God remain just and at the same time justify us? (Romans 3:26). Go and read the whole book of Romans, but especially chapters three and four to hear the answer to that question.

The answer is just simply the Cross. Like pilgrim in John Bunyan's great book, *Pilgrim's Progress*, we carry a burden which only comes off at the foot of the Cross. The recommended book below is John Stott's, *The Cross of Christ*. It is one of the clearest and most beautiful explanations of just how the Cross does this.

When you see the Cross and what it means; when you understand that it turns aside the wrath of God against sin, then you have the answer to the question – to what extent does God forgive? There is no sin which you have done which God cannot forgive. Not one. That is why John writes 'If we confess our sins, he is faithful and just and will forgive us all our sins, and purify us from all unrighteousness' (1 John 1:9). To what extent? Later on, John tells us; 'But if anybody does sin, we have an advocate with the Father—Jesus Christ, the Righteous One. He is the atoning sacrifice for our sins, and not only for ours but also for the sins of the whole world' (1 John 2:1-2).

In the words of the old hymn: 'There is a fountain filled with blood, drawn from Emmanuel's veins. And sinners cleansed beneath that flood, lose all their guilty stains.'

All. All. Every single one of them. There is no sin that you or I have committed which is too much for the remedy of the Cross to deal with.

Of course, as John points out, we have to admit our sins and to repent of them. If we don't accept we have sinned, we won't ask for forgiveness and God will not give us what we do not want. If we accept we have sinned, but think we can deal with it ourselves, we don't understand the depth or horror of our sin, and we commit the sin of seriously overestimating our abilities! And if we go to the opposite extreme of thinking our sin is too great for God, we are seriously underestimating the power of the Cross!

This is beautifully summed up in the simple but profound Gospel song 'He Paid a Debt He Did Not Owe' – the first verse of which is:

He paid a debt He did not owe; I owed a debt I could not pay.
I needed someone to wash my sins away.
And now I sing a brand new song: Amazing Grace. All day long.
Christ Jesus paid the debt that I could never pay.

Or since we are in song mode ...

Have you been to Jesus for the cleansing power?
Are you washed in the blood of the lamb?
Are you fully trusting in His grace this hour?
Are you washed in the blood of the lamb?

CONSIDER: To what extent do you think you need forgiveness? Ask God to make you aware of your sin. But at the same time make sure that you ask him to show you the extent of his forgiveness and the remedy he has provided. Given that he has forgiven us so much, how do you think that affects our forgiveness of others?

RECOMMENDED FURTHER READING:

The Cross of Christ – John Stott

Forgive – Tim Keller

PRAYER: Our Father in heaven, forgive us our debts, as we have also forgiven our debtors. Help us to see that as far as East is from the West, so far have you removed our sins from us (Psalm 103:12). We praise you for the sacrifice of Jesus – whose death cleanses us, pays for our sin and gives us eternal life. Hallelujah!

QUESTION: What would happen if God were not perfect?

BIBLE READING: Deuteronomy 32:1-6

TEXT: 'He is the Rock, his works are perfect, and all his ways are just. A faithful God who does no wrong, upright and just is he' (Deuteronomy 32:4).

If God were not perfect, we would be living in hell. The ancients believed in imperfect gods who raped, killed, abused and lied. No one really argues that the God of the Bible is like that – although Richard Dawkins does try. 'The God of the Old Testament is arguably the most unpleasant character in all fiction: jealous and proud of it; a petty, unjust, unforgiving control-freak; a vindictive, bloodthirsty ethnic cleanser; a misogynistic, homophobic, racist, infanticidal, genocidal, filicidal, pestilential, megalomaniacal, sadomasochistic, capriciously malevolent bully.' (*The God Delusion*)

Dawkins in his arrogance sets himself up against God, and in his ignorance displays a complete lack of understanding of what the Bible – both in the Old and New Testament – teaches about God. Deuteronomy 32:4 gives the lie to Dawkins' bombastic rant.

It is interesting that when Dawkins was doing tours to promote his book, when he read this paragraph, it was often greeted with cheers and shouts as though he were at an old-fashioned evangelistic rally. It's not that people were impressed with the reasoning, or the knowledge being displayed – they just loved the sentiment because they were operating under the new fundamentalist atheist motto, 'there is no God and I hate him'.

None of this is new. When the devil tempted Eve in the garden of Eden, he questioned both God's Word ('did God really say?') and his goodness (Genesis 3). The suggestion that God lied was matched by the suggestion that God wanted to keep something good from Adam and Eve. The devil is the father of lies. He has been lying from the beginning and he will continue to lie. The greatest lie of all is that God is not perfect. Perhaps the next is that the devil has convinced humanity that we are the ones who can determine the goodness and perfection of God. The arrogance of a fallen and flawed humanity thinking that we have the right, let alone the ability, to sit in judgement upon God, is stunning.

The question itself is not rational. It does not make sense. It's like asking what would happen if there was no gravity, or the colour blue didn't exist, or you didn't have a brain? There is gravity, blue does exist, and you do have a brain! It may be an interesting thought experiment to imagine the non-existence of what exists, but it is pointless. However, when we 'imagine' or listen to the lies of the Evil One it is not just a pointless thought experiment – it is blasphemous and harmful. To have evil thoughts of the Good God is itself evil.

We all think in parameters. Our ideas, morals, thoughts have boundaries. For example, I am writing this with the assumption that words make sense and that it is possible to communicate to other human beings. All of us operate with certain core beliefs that are fundamental to our thinking and existence. God gives us the parameters to use as we think of him. He is the ultimate communicator, and he has told us who he is. When I am trying to think through a difficult problem, or deal with doubts about anything I remind myself what the parameters are. God is good. God is sovereign. God is just. God is love. God's ways are perfect. All his ways are just. He does no wrong. Take away those and nothing makes sense.

But what about when things don't seem to make sense? What if something appears so manifestly unjust and wrong that it calls into question the goodness of God? Like the Cross? Was there ever anything more unjust and wrong than the crucifixion of the Son of God? And yet God meant it for good.

The problem is not with the goodness of God, it is with our limited understanding and perceptions. We limit the world and what is good to our understanding. Instead, we need to remember that 'in all things God works for the good of those who love him' (Romans 8:28).

Or to put it another way – we do not start with the imperfection of the world and our own imperfections and then move from them to question the perfection of God. We start with the perfection of God. To give that up is to walk into the ultimate darkness. I think of the woman who was so upset that I had referred to God as father. Why? Because her own father had abused her and so the image was understandably horrific. The solution? She needed to stop judging God by her father and instead judge her father by God.

Once we grasp that the perfection and goodness of God is not up for debate – we will be in the wonderful position of Job. 'though he slay me, yet will I hope in him' (Job 13:15).

CONSIDER: When the Accuser tempts you with accusations against God – what is the best way to respond? What will you base your life on – the goodness of God or the 'goodness' of humanity?

RECOMMENDED FURTHER READING:
The Good God – Mike Reeves

PRAYER: Read and pray Psalm 103 and/or Psalm 111. They are prayers and songs of praise that magnify the goodness of God.

41: SATAN, THE SNAKE AND HELL

QUESTION: Is hell or Satan real – if so, why did God create them? Why did God create the snake in the garden?

BIBLE READING: Revelation 20

TEXT: 'And the devil, who deceived them, was thrown into the lake of burning sulphur, where the beast and the false prophet had been thrown. They will be tormented day and night for ever and ever' (Revelation 20:10).

To answer the first part of your question simply. Yes, hell and Satan are real. If they were not then the Bible would be lying and none of it would make any sense.

This question is tied with the many other questions we ask on suffering (*ASK* 14, *SEEK* 4), evil, the devil (*SEEK* 29) and hell (*ASK* 18). We ask these questions because they are really important. The relationship between good and evil, God and the

171

devil, heaven and hell is vital to our understanding and well-being.

Why is that? Let's let Richard Dawkins explain – 'The universe that we observe has precisely the properties we should expect if there is, at bottom , no design, no purpose, no evil, no good, nothing but pitiless indifference.' (*River out of Eden*) If there is no God. If there is no design. If there is no evil and no good then we are left with a universe in which evil things happen, except they are not evil – because there is no evil. It's just blind, pitiless indifference. Isn't that a horrible world to live in – we could even call it hellish – except we are told there is no hell.

If you take away hell and the devil, you still have to deal with pain, suffering and yes – evil.

Which is exactly what the Bible does.

Can I suggest that you read through the book of Revelation? It is a difficult book (perhaps get Nancy Guthrie's *Blessed* to help) but it really does show how the cosmic battle between God and Satan plays out on the earth. It is far more realistic and real than the hopeless pitiless indifference of Dawkins.

Or take Colossians which explains first of all that Christ is the one who is in charge of all creation and that he is the one who holds everything together. That creation is disrupted by the devil and poisoned by evil. Which is why Jesus taught us to pray – 'deliver us from evil'. He did so when he 'disarmed the powers and authorities, he made a public spectacle of them, triumphing over them by the cross' (Colossians 2:15).

It is foolish not to believe in the devil. It is also foolish to be obsessed by him. C.S. Lewis in *The Screwtape Letters* explains 'There are two equal and opposite errors into which our race can fall about the devils. One is to disbelieve in their existence.

The other is to believe, and to feel an excessive and unhealthy interest in them. They themselves are equally pleased by both errors and hail a materialist or a magician with the same delight.' (*The Screwtape Letters* p. 8)

I have known people who blame everything bad that either happens to them, or is done by them, on the devil. Like the child who argued that she ate all the ice cream in the fridge because 'the devil made me do it'! That is not biblical. We still have human responsibility and are not just pawns in a game between God and the devil.

Remember that God and the devil are not equal. God is not created. The devil is. He is a created angel who has fallen and gone against his Creator. He seeks to destroy the Creation which is why he came in the form of a snake to deceive and disrupt that which God called 'very good'. Why did God create him? The simple answer is for the same reason that he created us – to glorify and enjoy him. Remember that God did not create the devil evil – but he did give him the opportunity to turn away and that is where evil comes from.

And yet still God is in control. And out of the great darkness brought on the earth comes an even greater good to overcome it. In order to choose and love God freely, we had to have a choice. In the providence and mercy of God, the rebellion of Satan, resulted in the fall of humanity, and ultimately the re-creation that comes through the life, death and resurrection of the Lord Jesus. Even the worst actions of the devil are turned for good by our Almighty Lord.

CONSIDER: Satan is real. Hell is real. It was made for him – not for you. All evil will be contained there for all eternity. Where would you rather be? With Christ in heaven or with the devil in hell? It should not be a difficult choice!

RECOMMENDED FURTHER READING:
Fear Not – What the Bible has to say about Angels, Demons, the Occult and Satan – Simon Van Bruchem
How Could a Loving God Send Anyone to Hell? – Benjamin M. Skaug

PRAYER: O Lord, we bless you that you have defeated the Dragon; that your truth exposes and destroys the lies of the Father of Lies; that the Serpent who deceived is on a chain, and will soon be able to deceive no more. Deliver us from the Evil One – and enable us to live for your glory and in your light and truth, Amen.

BIBLE READING: Psalm 8

TEXT: 'What is mankind that you are mindful of them, human beings that you care for them? You have made them a little lower than the angels and crowned them with glory and honour' (Psalm 8:4-5).

Have you heard of the VHEM movement? I suspect not. The acronym stands for Voluntary Human Extinction Movement. Founded by an American environmental activist, Les U. Knight it argues that human beings should cease to reproduce and so make ourselves extinct for the good of the planet. It goes without saying that Mr Knight does not share the biblical view of humanity or indeed the planet. The earth was created 'good' and humanity was the apex of that. Human beings were created to do precisely the opposite of Mr Knight's anti-human stance. We were to 'be fruitful and increase in number; fill the earth and subdue it' (Genesis 1:28).

But things went wrong. When given the choice to obey God and stay in fellowship with him, or try to be gods ourselves, we chose the latter. As a result, humanity fell, and the creation has been suffering the impact ever since. In Genesis 6 God told Noah 'I am going to put an end to all people, for the earth is filled with violence because of them. I am surely going to destroy both them and the earth' (Genesis 6:13). He also 'regretted that he had made human beings on the earth, and his heart was deeply troubled' (Genesis 6:6). That is such an extraordinary verse. If the VHEM movement was seeking biblical justification this would surely be their verse!

But God so loved the world that he found a way to deal with our sin and rebellion, and to create a new heavens and a new earth. He gave us his Son who came as a human being to save human beings.

Why did God create human beings? Did he need us? Paul answered that question when he was speaking to the Athenian philosophers – 'The God who made the world and everything in it is the Lord of heaven and earth and does not live in temples built by hands. And he is not served by human hands, as if he needed anything, because he himself gives all men life and breath and everything else' (Acts 17:24-25). God created us because he wanted to. But how did he create us?

Let's return to the Shorter Catechism – this time Question 10.

Q: How did God create man?
A: God created man male and female, after his own image, in knowledge, righteousness,and holiness, with dominion over the creatures. Genesis 1:27: 'So God created man in his own image, in the image of God he created him; male and female he created them.'

We are made in God's image. We are made to be stewards of the rest of his Creation - not to destroy it, but to control it for good. We were made for God. As Augustine put it - 'Our hearts were made for you, and they are restless until they find our rest in you.'

This is such a high view of humanity. Mr Knight and his colleagues have the low view of human beings that results from an atheistic perspective which ultimately ends up in seeing humans as little more than sophisticated parasites - a blot on the earth - which would be well rid of us.

But the Bible has such a high view. We are 'fearfully and wonderfully made' (Psalm 139:14). We are made a little lower than the angels, and crowned in glory and honour (Psalm 8). Even more amazingly humanity is redeemed by the Creator becoming one of us. This is what we call the incarnation - God coming in a human body. God becoming a human being. He didn't come as a mouse or a mountain - he came as a man!

Can you see how practical and important this is in today's world, in your life? Every human is made in the image of God. Every human is made for God. That is the foundation of the principle of equality. Secular humanism - that is humanism without God - has no basis for equality. It just borrows the Christian fruit, but rejects the root from which that fruit comes. Christian humanism recognises the glory and honour of humanity because we recognise the glory and honour of the God in whose image we are made.

God made us for his glory. Back to the catechism – question 1. 'What is man's chief end?' (i.e. Why were we made? What is our purpose?). 'Man's chief end is to glorify God and enjoy him forever'. You can't beat that!

CONSIDER: Can you think of other practical implications of the teaching about humanity that the Bible brings? How should it make you see other people? And yourself?

RECOMMENDED FURTHER READING:
What is Man? – A. Craig Troxel
What Makes us Human? – Mark Meynell

PRAYER: LORD, our Lord, how majestic is your name in all the earth! ... When I consider your heavens, the work of your fingers, the moon and the stars, which you have set in place, what is mankind that you are mindful of them, human beings that you care for them? You have made them a little lower than the angels and crowned them with glory and honour ... LORD, our Lord, how majestic is your name in all the earth! (Psalm 8:1, 3-5, 9).

43. THE CHURCH AND WOMEN

QUESTION: Is the Church an outdated Patriarchal institution? What does the Bible say about women in the Church? What if women were created first? Why is God male?

BIBLE READING: Romans 16

TEXT: 'I commend to you our sister Phoebe, a deacon of the church in Cenchreae. I ask you to receive her in the Lord in a way worthy of his people and to give her any help she may need from you, for she has been the benefactor of many people, including me' (Romans 16:1-2).

It's funny how the language and ideas of the culture so permeate the Church that sometimes we take their assumptions and assume that they are true. We are told something like 'the Church is an outdated Patriarchal institution?' and we either believe it, or try to show that we are not – by using the criteria and assumptions of the culture.

I don't accept any of the premises in the accusation – it is an accusation rather than a question. The Church of Jesus Christ is never outdated – we follow the one who is the same yesterday, today and forever. We follow the one whose words will never pass away. Our societies will have changing fashions – but we have the unchanging Word. Which is not to say that there have not been individual churches or Christians who have had a misogynistic view of women. There still are. I have come across that in many contexts. But just because some people misuse Scripture to justify their wrong cultural beliefs, that does not mean we should jettison Scripture in order to justify our wrong cultural beliefs.

The Bible clearly teaches that the human race is male and female – and that both are made in the image of God. The fact that Adam was created first does not mean that the man is superior. The fact that Eve was second does not mean a woman is just a spare rib! But one of the consequences of the Fall has been conflict and discordant relationships between the sexes.

The Bible also clearly teaches – and nature/science shows us – that there are differences between men and women. We are equal but different. We complement one another. In different human societies those differences can be expressed in different ways – and sometimes in ways that are sinful and wrong. But to deny the differences is to deny reality and to cause harm.

When Jesus came into the world his purpose was not just to redeem individuals but to break down those things that divide us. He chose twelve male disciples to be his apostles, but he was also happy to have women amongst his followers. As passages like 1 Timothy 3 indicate the early Church followed the pattern of Jesus – and appointed only men as elders. Although they did have women as deacons and women, unusually for the time, fully participated in the church services of worship, and the life of the Church. When we look at the teaching of Paul in Romans 16 note how many women he publicly commends. Phoebe was a deaconess of the Church, Priscilla was a hard worker (note how she is mentioned before her husband); Mary worked very hard as did Tryphena and Tryphosa, Persis and Rufus's mother, not to forget Julia and Nereus's sister. There is no hint of inferiority here.

The Bible has plenty to say about the role of women and men in the Church. It is obviously a subject that is of great interest (and confusion) in today's Church – as we seek to avoid both the cultural bias of previous generations and this one. I can recall announcing that I was going to preach on the role of women in the Church, home and society. The evening I did so one of the elders came to me before the service and said 'Boy, you are in trouble'! Why? 'The congregation has doubled'. Why was that a bad thing? The whole feminist society from the University had turned up! We actually had a great night as we looked at what the Word of God had to say on the subject. At the end one young woman came up to me and pleaded: 'Please can you do the same for the men? They really need it'. So, we did.

I would strongly suggest that you read either Claire Smith's or Kevin DeYoung's books on the subject. They are extremely helpful.

In terms of the last two parts of your question. God didn't create the woman first so the question does not really matter –

given that we have already been told that men and women are equally in the image of God. And God is not male. Have a look at *ASK* 11 for the answer to the question 'which gender is God'?

CONSIDER: If you are female what difference does it make to you to know what the Bible teaches about being a woman? If you are male what difference does it make to you? What do you think are the differences between men and women? And what are the similarities? Can you think of ways that your culture or Church might get it wrong?

RECOMMENDED FURTHER READING:

God's Good Design: What the Bible Really Says About Men and Women – Claire Smith
Men and Women in the Church – Kevin DeYoung
God's Design for Women – Biblical Womanhood for Today – Sharon James

PRAYER: Lord Jesus, we praise your name that you came to save both men and women. That in you there is ultimately neither male nor female but we are all one. We ask forgiveness when sometimes we have misused the teaching from your Word about men and women. Help us to treat one another as brothers and sisters. Give us the courage to challenge abuse when we see it – and grant your grace, love and unity to all the family of God. Amen.

44 EVANGELISM – WHY?

QUESTION: Should you evangelise? How do you evangelise?

BIBLE READING: Matthew 25:31-46

TEXT: 'Then they will go away to eternal punishment, but the righteous to eternal life' (Matthew 25:46).

Who wants to be an evangelist? Who wants to be evangelised? With many people the term evangelism has a negative and somewhat weird connotation. It conjures up images of someone standing on the street corner yelling out 'repent or die' at passing strangers. Or a Billy Graham type figure in a vast stadium encouraging people to come forward and be saved. Or perhaps you think of the slightly eccentric person whose zeal you admire but who you don't really want to sit beside you in church?!

Why does evangelism have such a bad rap? What is evangelism? It is the telling of the 'evangel' – the good news about Jesus. According to the Oxford English dictionary it is 'the spreading of the Christian gospel by public preaching or personal witness.' Or 'zealous advocacy or support of a particular cause.' It is the latter definition which often causes the discomfort.

I recently saw a job advert for a 'home work evangelist'. As I describe myself as an evangelist and as it had a salary of $200,000, I was curious! It turns out that this was nothing to do with the good news of Jesus Christ, but was rather about the 'good news' of being able to work from home. It is interesting that in contemporary society it is acceptable to be a 'climate evangelist' or a 'music evangelist', or a 'home work evangelist', but being an evangelist of Jesus Christ is often met with derision, fear and abuse.

Why should we seek to tell people about Jesus?

He tells us to. If we are followers of Christ, we do what he asks. And he commands his Church to 'go and make disciples of all nations' (Matthew 28:19). We are part of that Church – and until he returns again that will be our task. You are here on this earth to be witnesses of Christ.

People are lost – Those who are without Christ are 'without hope and without God in the world' (Ephesians 2:12). Jesus says that those who do not believe are 'condemned already' (John 3:18). And he leaves us in no doubt what that means – they are destined for an eternity without him. They are hell bound. They are lost.

'One wonders how much of Christianity's power to win the world has been crippled by the modern fashion of denying or ignoring the reality of hell. It is certainly a fashion rather than a proof or a discovery. Both reason and faith inform us of hell: reason, because it is irrational to think that souls created free to refuse God can be compelled to accept him; faith, because if no one goes to hell, then Jesus is a liar or a fool, for he more than anyone warned against it.' Peter Kreeft (*Christianity for Modern Pagans* - p. 178).

What kind of heartless and cruel people would we have to be if we see people heading for such destruction and in such a condition and yet we do nothing about it. Especially when we know the Christ who came to seek and to save the lost? How can people believe unless they hear? 'How, then, can they call on the one they have not believed in? And how can they believe in the one of whom they have not heard? And how can they hear without someone preaching to them?' (Romans 10:14).

The glory of God - Whenever a sinner is saved it brings glory to God - because only God can do it. Jesus endured the Cross because it would bring him joy (Hebrews 12:2) - the joy of seeing a great multitude saved and brought to heaven.

It grows our own faith in Christ - Paul tells Philemon to be active in sharing his faith so that his understanding of 'every good thing we have in Christ' would be deepened (Philemon 6). I find that sharing the Gospel about Jesus and seeing him work through his Spirit so that his Word does not return to him empty, is such a great encouragement to my faith and understanding.

The good of the world – If you are concerned about the planet and your fellow human beings then you will want to see people become Christians. Did you know that the whole creation is eagerly waiting for the children of God to be revealed? (Romans 8:19). It is only when we are set free that the creation will be liberated from its bondage to decay. If you want to save the planet – do evangelism!

CONSIDER: Why do you think some Christians do not want to evangelise? Can you think of any other reasons to reach out with the Gospel? When was the last time you shared the good news about Jesus with anyone?

RECOMMENDED FURTHER READING:

Erasing Hell – Francis Chan and Preston Sprinkle
Christianity for Modern Pagans – Peter Kreeft

PRAYER: O Lord Jesus, we confess to you with sorrow that we are so slow to share the good news of what you have done for people. You suffered, bled and died for us. You ask us to be your witnesses and yet we are reluctant, we are embarrassed. Fill us with your love. Fill us with your Spirit. Give us your heart. And enable us to have the beautiful feet of those who share the Gospel. For your glory. Amen.

45. EVANGELISM – HOW?

BIBLE READING: 1 Peter 3:13-16

TEXT: 'But in your hearts revere Christ as Lord. Always be prepared to give an answer to everyone who asks you to give the reason for the hope that you have. But do this with gentleness and respect' (1 Peter 3:15).

The last chapter dealt with why we should evangelise – in this one we look at the second part of your question – how do we evangelise?

It's such a difficult question – and one which I think about every day – because it is my job. Every time I go to a school, I think about how I can share the Good News with teenagers who in this hopeless world, desperately need to hear it. When I go to work, near the University of Sydney, sometimes I sit in a café outside and watch all the students walking past and reflect on how

I could tell these students the Good News? And what about my neighbours – Muslims, Hindus, Buddhists, nominal Christians, atheists and agnostics? Or those of my relatives and friends who are not Christians?

I want to share the Good News, but I don't want to force religion upon them, or offend them, or put them off! Sometimes it feels that it is so difficult that we are tempted to say 'Lord, can't I just leave it to you to let them know?'. It's easy for some of us as Christians to hide behind the sovereignty of God. We believe that God is in charge of everything, and that he will do his own will, so we leave him to it. But that doesn't really work because his will is to use us to share the Good News. Of course, we cannot convert anyone. That is the job of the Holy Spirit. But the Holy Spirit uses means. He uses us.

How do we evangelise? First of all we need to remember what evangelism is not. It's not a sales programme. In fact, it's not a programme at all. Evangelism is about people not projects. It is pointing people to Jesus. People are not projects – and they are not data to be manipulated or signed up to make us feel good that we have had so many converts.

In a short book I wrote called *Engaging with Atheists* I suggested the following principles for engaging personally which I hope you will find helpful.

1. Listen and Learn – the first rule of communication is to listen – really listen. This will avoid you making wrong assumptions about the people you are talking to.
2. Question and Think – ask good questions of those you are talking to.
3. Read and Watch – It's important to understand the culture we are all swimming in – through books, magazines, the Internet, films, podcasts etc.

4. Communicate – In a saying, falsely attributed to Francis of Assisi but endlessly repeated as profound wisdom, we are told 'preach the Gospel at all times, use words if necessary'. This is nonsense. Imagine you want to tell your girlfriend you love her and want to marry her – do you not think words are necessary? Of course, words without actions are often meaningless, but then so are actions without words.

5. Begin where people are – what is your starting point? Once you find out where people are in terms of their beliefs, then you can help them to see where the end point is. Show them that there really is the possibility of a much better (eternal) future for them.

6. Love – love means that you treat people the way you want to be treated. Love means that you are patient, looking for the best of the person you are speaking to, that you are for real, that you don't lie, manipulate, or deceive. Love means most of all that you point them to the God who is love.

7. Pray – it's good to talk to people about Jesus. It's even better to talk to Jesus about people.

8. Use the Bible – it is the Word of God that is living and effective. It is through the living and enduring Word of God that we are born again (1 Peter 1:23). It's not the Gospel unless it's the Gospel.

9. Leave it – in other words don't be too pushy. You don't have to say everything in one go.

10. Together – the lone evangelist is not good. Jesus sent his disciples out in twos. And it was to the Church that he gave his great commission.

Whilst it is good to memorise Scripture, I'm not so sure it is good to memorise a formula - because I don't think the Gospel can be reduced to a formula or a set of rules. Think of it like a diamond. A diamond can have a thousand different reflections depending on the light that shines on it, and the perception of the viewer. Likewise with Christ - his beauty is dazzling from any angle - our job is to proclaim him as he is taught in his Word and as we know him in our own lives. In fact, the best way to evangelise is surely this - get to know other people better - and most of all get to know Jesus better. You cannot communicate what you do not know.

CONSIDER: Paul tells us that 'to the one we are an aroma that brings death; to the other, an aroma that brings life. And who is equal to such a task?' (2 Corinthians 2:16). This tells us of the different reactions we may have - and our weakness. We need the Holy Spirit. Have a look at the parable of the sower as well to see how this all works out (Matthew 13:1-23).

RECOMMENDED FURTHER READING:
Engaging with Atheists - David Robertson
Evangelism and the Sovereignty of God - J.I. Packer
Making Faith Magnetic - Daniel Strange

PRAYER: O Lord give us wisdom, grace, love and the communication skills we need as we seek to share the Good News with our friends, family, schoolmates, work colleagues, neighbours and strangers. Command what you will and give what you command, in your name. Amen.

BIBLE READING: John 16:1-15

TEXT: 'But very truly I tell you, it is for your good that I am going away. Unless I go away, the Advocate will not come to you; but if I go, I will send him to you' (John 16:7).

It sounds logical doesn't it. Given what we have just seen in the past chapter about evangelism – would it not be so much easier if Jesus was here on earth? How many would flock to see him? The most people I have ever heard gathered to listen to someone speak was when Jordan Peterson came to Sydney in 2022. A sell-out crowd of 9,000 hung on his every word (and there were plenty of them!). Imagine what crowds we would draw if Jesus went on tour!

But that's not what Jesus thought. In fact, he told the disciples, who I suspect did not immediately grasp how this could be true, that it would be better for them if he went away.

Why would it be better?

Let's return to my going to hear Jordan Peterson at the Sydney Exhibition Centre. We got to see him, projected on a screen from a distance and to hear him. A lucky few got to ask him questions through the Slido technology. A handful got to go backstage and meet with him afterwards. I was thankful to be part of that handful. But he was limited in his time, in his body and mind (he was really tired). It was great to chat briefly with him, but he is not the Messiah!

Imagine if Jesus was like that? Limited to a human body on earth – only able to give a few minutes to a few people. Would we really want him to give access only to those who could afford the tickets?

The Ascension of Jesus is a much-neglected topic. Even for someone like me who has been a Christian for forty-five years it was only a couple of years ago that I grasped something of the practical difference it makes. There are not many books I would regard as life changing – but Gerrit Scott Dawson's *Jesus Ascended* was one such book. Amongst other things I learned the answers to the following questions:

1. Is Jesus still human? Yes – he still has a human body. But it is a renewed body. A different kind of human body – one that we shall have. One that is free from the bondage to decay we currently experience. He doesn't get tired or weary. As 'Rabbi' Duncan put it: 'the dust of the earth sits on the throne of heaven'.

2. Where is he? Dawson cites Calvin's wise comments.

'What? Do we place Christ midway among the spheres? Or do we build him a cottage among the planets? Heaven, we regard as the magnificent palace of God, far outstripping all this world's fabric'. (Dawson p. 40).

3.   What is he doing? He is sending his Word as the prophet; he is praying as our priest, and he is reigning as our King. And he is with us. He is present with us through his Spirit. Where two or three are gathered he is there in the midst. When we gather in worship we can honestly stand up and tell people 'Jesus is here ... Jesus is in the house!' When we sit at his table, he is not absent – he is present with us – which is why the Lord's Supper is so much more than a memorial to absent friends!

Another way to think of this is that he is giving us, his Church, gifts. Paul cites Psalm 68:18 to the Ephesians to prove this – 'When he ascended on high, he took many captives and gave gifts to his people' (Ephesians 4:8).

As to your specific question regarding witness. It is because he has given us these great gifts – his Word, Spirit and Church, that we are able to bear witness to the end of the earth. He has not left us alone. He is present with us.

'We have gained in Christ more than we lost in Adam' (Dawson p. 71). Let me add to that. We have gained more from Christ ascending than we would have if he had remained on earth.

CONSIDER: Isn't it an amazing – and to be honest sometimes quite scary – that Jesus is with us? He is not with us like a Zoom call. It's far more than that. You don't have to dial him up and wait until he answers. He is with us always. He's not with us in a physical sense – it's far better than that. He is with us by his Spirit, in his Church, Word and Sacraments. What are the practical implications of all of this for you if you are a believer? And if you are not a believer, why would you not want this?

RECOMMENDED FURTHER READING:

Jesus Ascended – Gerrit Scott Dawson

The Ascension: Humanity in the Presence of God by Tim Chester and Jonny Woodrow.

The Ascension of Christ – Patrick Schreiner

PRAYER: Dear Lord Jesus Christ, right before your Ascension into heaven you told your apostles to be His witnesses to the ends of the earth upon receiving the Holy Spirit. May I be similarly inspired to spread your Gospel message in word and deed, according to your will for me. And may I do so prudently and joyfully, with your help, your guidance, and your grace! And remembering this glorious event, help me to seek what is above, heaven, where you are seated at the right hand of God the Father! (I found this beautiful prayer on a Catholic website)

BIBLE READING: Hebrews 10:1-18

TEXT: 'For by one sacrifice he has made perfect forever those who are being made holy' (Hebrews 10:14).

Several young people have asked this question. It is not an easy one to answer without offending or confusing people, because people are approaching it from different perspectives. For example, you seem to be assuming in your question that being Catholic is different from being a Christian. That may be true in your personal circumstances, but it is not a rule you can make for everyone.

I personally know several fine Catholic Christians – for example the author and journalist Greg Sheridan whose book *Christians, the Urgent Case for Jesus in our World* I would highly recommend. I love reading Catholic writers like G.K. Chesterton,

Pascal, Aquinas and Augustine. One of the best modern Christian writers is Peter Kreeft (see question 44 for my recommendation of one of his books). In the last question I cited a prayer I got from a Catholic website. Some of the finest and most devout believers I have known are Catholics. And I confess that I have spoken in Catholic churches (usually on abortion). On the other hand, I have also known plenty of people whose family are Protestant, yet they themselves are not Christians. In fact, on both Catholic and Protestant sides there are plenty who are cultural Christians – their Christianity is not tied in with their personal faith in Christ but which cultural religious tribe they belong to. That can be true for those who take the label 'evangelical' to describe themselves. For example one survey in the U.S. found that one third of 'evangelicals' did not agree with the Trinity, a fundamental doctrine of the Christian faith.

I also know many former Catholics who are now in Protestant churches and who struggle with the idea that someone can be a Catholic and remain in the Roman Catholic Church (some of this is dependent on the culture of the country they come from).

This does not mean that Catholic and Protestant churches are just two sides of the same coin or that the distinctions between us don't matter. There has been a bit of a trend in recent years to see some evangelical Christians 'crossing the Tiber' (another way of saying that they have joined the Roman Catholic Church).

Sometimes I am asked, given that I have a lot of time for some Catholic teachings, Catholic philosophers, and especially their social theology (for example unlike some Protestant churches they are strongly opposed to abortion and to same sex marriage, and for justice for the poor) – why I have not done the same.

There are some Catholic doctrines that I just cannot believe. For example, they believe in Purgatory (a place where Christians go after they have died in order to get their sins purged and to be purified – Christ has already done that for me!). Then there is the aspect of praying to Mary or to the Saints – why do that when we can pray directly to Jesus? I also believe that whilst the Church is important, and the confessions and history of the Church are to be greatly valued, our ultimate authority always has to be the Word of God, the Bible.

It is impossible for me to believe that the Pope is the head of the Church. I don't believe, like some Protestants that the Pope is the anti-Christ, and I am greatly appreciative of the writings for example of Pope Benedict, but I do know that the behaviour of some Popes has been atrocious. The infallibility of the Pope is an absurd doctrine – and I suspect many Catholics will come to believe that given the pronouncements of the current Pope Francis!

Another area of great difficulty is that of the Mass. I do not believe in what is called transubstantiation – the belief that the bread and wine are literally turned into the physical body and blood of Jesus. I do not believe that when we take communion, we are offering Christ as a sacrifice again (see the Hebrews text above). A few years ago, I was invited to meet with the new Catholic Archbishop of Edinburgh. I greatly enjoyed meeting with him and discussing in what areas we could co-operate. At one point he asked me – 'If I invited you to take Mass with me in my chapel, what would you say?' I told him that I would politely decline because I did not believe what he believed about the Mass, and He said, 'Good! You have no idea how many Protestants pastors have said to me that they would do it. But if they can take Mass they should be in the Catholic Church.

You and I can disagree but respect one another's position.' My position exactly.

The real problems for me occur not with Catholic doctrine about Christ but rather about what theologians call 'soteriology'. How we become Christians. Sadly, far too many Catholics believe in baptismal regeneration – that is they think that because they have been baptised they are saved. This leads to complacency and a type of religion which ends up being without Christ. This is not to undermine the importance of baptism but rather to say that baptism without faith in Christ, ultimately, whether that comes before or after the baptism, is not the important issue and does not save us.

And neither do good works. To put it simply. Protestants believe that we are saved by faith alone – we call it justification by faith. Catholics believe that it is a combination of faith and works. Although Protestants also believe that saving faith is never alone – and will always be evidenced by works. The distinctions may seem small – but in practice they are really substantial.

My Catholic friends want me to repent and come 'back' to what they consider to be 'Mother' Church – if not the only Church. I think that the Roman Catholic Church is a Christian Church, but that in some ways it has seriously erred. I suspect that they think the same way about me. I guess in heaven we will find out! But meanwhile I suggest that you 'search the Scriptures'.

CONSIDER: If you are a Christian in a traditional Catholic home, where you see little evidence of a living faith in Christ, consider how you can be a faithful and effective witness for Christ. Do the same if you are in a traditional Protestant home. Think about some of the differences mentioned above. Which are the most important?

RECOMMENDED FURTHER READING:
Nothing in my Hand I Bring - Ray Galea
A Christian's Pocket Guide to Papacy - Leonardo De Chirico
Jesus of Nazereth - Pope Benedict XVI

Here is a debate I did with Peter Williams on this subject for the Unbelievable programme - https://theweeflea. com/2022/09/11/should-we-all-join-the-roman-catholic-church-debate-with-peter-d-williams/

PRAYER: Lord Jesus, we praise your Name that you offered yourself as the one and only, unrepeatable sacrifice for our sins. We thank you that you are our great High Priest, and we don't need another one. You are the Head of the Church and you have given us your infallible Word, not fallible men. We thank you that you save people from every different religious background. May we never rely on our denomination, our church, our works, for salvation, but grant that we would trust solely in you. And grant that we would be united with all who share that same faith, in the name of the Father, the Son and the Holy Spirit. Amen.

48. CHRISTIANS DISUNITED

QUESTION: If all Christians believe in one God, how come they disagree a lot and divided themselves up into groups and they fight a lot and even kill each other sometimes?

BIBLE READING: John 17:20-26

TEXT: 'I have given them the glory that you gave me, that they may be one as we are one – I in them and you in me – so that they may be brought to complete unity. Then the world will know that you have sent me and have loved them even as you have loved me' (John 17:22-23).

Christian disunity is real. And it is really embarrassing, because we are all supposed to be united in one family, all sharing the love of Christ. 'There is one body and one Spirit, just as you were called to one hope when you were called; one Lord, one faith, one baptism; one God and

Father of all, who is over all and through all and in all'
(Ephesians 4:4-6).

So, what has gone wrong?

Let's start with your question about Christians killing
one another. This rarely happens. In the last question we
talked about cultural Christians – that is those who claim
a Christianity identity because of their tribe or country. So
sometimes you get people saying because I am Greek, I am
Christian (Orthodox), or because I am Irish, I am Christian
(Catholic), or because I am American, I am Christian
(Protestant). This is often a form of religious identity but
not Christianity. Or perhaps it is better to say that it is
Christianity without Christ. Christ does not tell us to kill
one another in his Name. Indeed, he forbids it. He goes even
further than that – he tells us that we are to love our enemies
and do good to those who hate us (Matthew 5:43-45). How
can we say that we are Christians if we do not follow Christ.

But that is not to say that true Christians never disagree
with one another. We are a family. I don't know about your
family, but my family often disagrees. Of course, I would want
my parents, wife, children and other relatives to recognise
that I am always right, but that isn't the way it is or should
be! Likewise, within the Christian Church there can be great
divisions which are more often caused by personality and
smaller matters.

Take, for example, the disagreement between Euodia and
Syntyche in the Philippian church. Paul had to appeal to them
to agree with one another (Philippians 4:2). It is possible
he even wrote his great poem/hymn on the humility and
suffering of Christ in chapter 2, because of them. We don't

know what their quarrel was, but I suspect it was relatively minor, perhaps whose house should the church meet in? I heard one old minister refer to them as 'Odious' and 'Soon Touchy'. That may have been harsh, but the point was well made. Much division is to do with our own sensitivities and sinfulness.

Sometimes there are more serious issues. Money and power can be great sources of division, especially when people forget who it is we are supposed to be serving: Christ, his Church and the poor.

But sometimes we do have to disagree. Because there can be harmful heresies and practices that come into the Church. The leaders of the church are called 'under shepherds' - because the Shepherd is of course Jesus. However, the leaders are to follow Jesus' example and teach and protect the flock. When a wolf comes in, they are to drive it away. Paul warned the Ephesian elders with tears that 'savage wolves will come in among you and will not spare the flock. Even from your own number men will arise and distort the truth in order to draw away disciples after them. So be on your guard!' (Acts 20:28-31).

'The greatest menace to the Christian Church today comes not from the enemies outside, but from the enemies within; it comes from the presence within the Church of a type of faith and practice that is anti-Christian to the core' (J. Gresham Machen - *Christianity and Liberalism* p. 135)

Each generation has to fight this battle. Because the unity of the Church which Jesus prays for so movingly in John 17 is dependent on our unity in Christ. When someone teaches a different gospel, or a different Christ - or denies the true Gospel by their actions - they must be opposed.

But we need to be careful not to pick fights for the sake of it, or over secondary or trivial issues. Even when we are dealing with the most important, we should heed the advice of Paul to Timothy: 'Opponents must be gently instructed, in the hope that God will grant them repentance leading them to a knowledge of the truth' (2 Timothy 2:25).

CONSIDER: This question is so important and a great reminder to us that Jesus prayed for the unity of his Church and his people. However, given the fact that we are all sinners, it is astonishing just how much unity there actually is in the Church. I feel united with lots of Christians from many different cultures and denominations. I was pastor of a church with people from a wide variety of backgrounds, different personalities and different views about many things. Yet, although we had disagreements, there was a basic, fundamental and deep unity. Nothing can explain that except the love and power of Christ. Let us pray that that would be our common experience and disunity would be our strange experience!

RECOMMENDED FURTHER READING:
Evangelical Truth – A personal plea for unity, integrity and faithfulness – John Stott
Christianity and Liberalism – J. Gresham Machen

PRAYER: Father, we echo the prayer of our Saviour Jesus. May we be one as you are one. May we be in you. May we be brought to complete unity. Then the world will know that you sent your Son and that you have loved us, and you love him. Amen.

49. SINNING CHRISTIANS

QUESTION: How come Christians say they are holy and yet they keep sinning? (Some even sin more than us who are not Christians?)

BIBLE READING: 1 John 1:5-10

TEXT: 'If we claim to be without sin, we deceive ourselves and the truth is not in us' (1 John 1:8).

This is again an important question. I have to say how impressed I am at the quality of questions you have all been asking. But this one is particularly important because sometimes one of the greatest obstacles to people thinking Christianity is for real, is the hypocrisy of some Christians. It's not just the ones we get in the media (and the media love to report the bad news about Christians – I once knew a hotel owner who was paid by a newspaper to report any bad story about a church person!), but also what we see for ourselves.

I was a pastor for six years in the beautiful Highland village of Brora. It may have been beautiful, but it too was full of sinners! One time a man came up to me and said 'I won't come to your church, because it's full of hypocrites' ... Perhaps I should not have replied the way I did. 'You're right, but you should come along. You would fit right in!'. I did apologise and asked him, 'Do you know any who are not?' And it's funny but every time I asked that question I got the same answer – 'Yes, there's Rossie and Angus, and Big Margaret and Wee Margaret and Big Donald and Sanders and ...' These were Christians who of course were still sinners, but they lived a life that was consistent and in keeping with their testimony.

A real Christian will not claim to be holier than thou! In fact, the more you grow as a Christian the more you are conscious of your own sin and weakness so that like the Apostle Paul towards the end of his life, you can honestly say 'I am the worst of sinners' (1 Timothy 1:15).

However, we do claim to be 'saints' in the biblical sense of the word. It literally means 'the holy ones'. We are holy, which means set apart for God, not because we are good but because Christ died to make us holy (Ephesians 5:25-26).

So, if that is the case, why do we still sin? Because although we are saved, we are not yet in heaven. We are not yet fully made holy (what is called sanctified). However, we are being made holy. There was an old T-shirt which summed it up well, 'Be patient with me. God has not finished with me yet'.

Also, there is something called 'common grace'. That is God's grace that works in all human beings. It is because of his mercy that we are not consumed. Whilst every human being is a sinner, every human being is also made in the image of God and retains something of that goodness. So, I am not surprised that you have met people who behave better and seem much nicer than many Christians – because I certainly have. I don't assume that because someone is a Christian that they are necessarily a better person than someone who isn't. Nonetheless none of us are saved by our good works, because they can never be good enough. It doesn't matter if we fall short by one per cent or by 100 per cent – we all fall short of the glory of God.

The real question is what we can do about sin? John tells us in the passage we read. First, we must not deceive ourselves by claiming to be without sin – we are not that holy. Then we need to confess our sins to Jesus – who because he is faithful and just will forgive us. It is his blood that purifies us from all sin. Knowing that we are forgiven gives us a great incentive to deal with our ongoing sin. Knowing that when we get it wrong, we have an advocate with the Father, Jesus Christ, the Righteous One, who is the atoning sacrifice for our sins (and for the sins of the whole world) is a great encouragement. With this knowledge we can be for real ... and holy and humble.

The point is not that the Christian is sinless, but that the Christian has someone who can deal with their sin. That is not the case for the non-Christian. Actually, that's wrong. The non-Christian does have someone who can deal with their sin, but they need to turn to him and repent and believe in him. Have you? Will you?

CONSIDER: There is an old hymn which has these lovely lines, 'There is a fountain filled with blood, drawn from Immanuel's veins; and sinners plunged beneath that flood, lose all their guilty stains' (Cowper). If you want forgiveness – from everything – that is where you must go. Come to the Cross. Come to Christ. And you will be forgiven.

RECOMMENDED FURTHER READING:

How Do I Kill Remaining Sin? – Geoff Thomas (a short 32 page book – but invaluable)
Gentle and Lowly – The Heart of Christ for Sufferers and Sinners – Dane Ortlund

PRAYER: 'Have mercy on me, O God, according to your unfailing love; according to your great compassion blot out my transgressions. Wash away all my iniquity and cleanse me from my sin' (Psalm 51:1–2).

50. GAY CHRISTIANS

QUESTION: How can you be Christian and gay? I love God very much and I want to grow my faith, but I can't change my preference on which gender I like. (It's like saying to a heterosexual, to go and love the same sex. They wouldn't).

BIBLE READING: 1 Corinthians 6:9-20

TEXT: 'Do you not know that your bodies are temples of the Holy Spirit, who is in you, whom you have received from God? You are not your own; you were bought at a price. Therefore honour God with your bodies' (1 Corinthians 6:19-20).

Many people feel the way you do. It is sometimes difficult to work out what is right and wrong when what we desire seems to conflict with what we believe.

It is a fundamental dogma of our society that sexuality is all important, unchangeable and must be expressed. It is regarded as the most basic of human rights. On the other hand, Jesus clearly teaches that marriage is between a man and a woman and that sex outside marriage is wrong (see *ASK* 33). Given those views your question is understandable. There is a conflict between the teaching of our culture, and the teaching of Christ. For some Christians that creates a dilemma. However, it shouldn't, not on this or any other issue where the Bible gives us clear teaching. Who should we obey? Christ or men?

There is another issue here. Your question seems to be written with the presuppositions of our culture. You are same sex attracted and you think that in order to be a Christian you have to change to become opposite sex attracted. That presupposes that our feelings are the ultimate authority in what should guide our behaviour. They are not. We put ourselves at the centre of the Universe and as the source of right and wrong. But we are not the Creator – we are creatures. We don't get to make our own rules. We follow the Maker's instructions.

Sometimes I describe myself as an IKEA Christian. In case you have never had the dubious pleasure of visiting an IKEA store it is the large well-known Swedish furniture chain, and purveyor of meatballs, where you collect Scandinavian style flatpack furniture, go home and assemble it yourself. They give you detailed instructions so that people like me, who are useless with their hands, can assemble the bookshelf – or whatever else you have bought. As I do not have a practical bone in my body, I do what they say. I lay out all the pieces and follow the step-by-step guidelines. I follow the maker's instructions. Do you not think that we should follow our Maker's instructions?

But what are these? If I can set it out in these steps.

1. God is our Maker.
2. He made us sexual beings.
3. He tells us that sex is to be within marriage and that marriage is between a man and a woman. Anything outside of that is sin.
4. Sex is not just an appetite to be indulged as we see fit.
5. Sex or marriage is not essential to being a human being. After all Jesus was the only perfect human being and he was not married (whatever novels like the Da Vinci may say!).
6. The Bible's teaching on sex and marriage provides for the good of society, the good of the family and the good of individuals. If we go against it – it is a bit like putting diesel fuel into a petrol driven car – it won't work.

I'm pretty sure that you are smart enough to work out the implications of all that. Think about it from a different context. If I said that I am a Christian, but I feel attracted to lots of different women (or men), therefore I should be allowed to sleep with lots of different people, because that is the way I am made, what would you say?

As a Christian, I may find myself 'liking' lots of different people, but that does not give me the right to disobey the Maker's instructions. As Paul told the Corinthians, who were also faced with society and personal pressures, we are to 'flee from sexual immorality' because our bodies are 'a temple of the Holy Spirit' who is in us, and who we have received from God. We are not our own, we were bought with a price (1 Corinthians 6:18-20).

There are some people who don't accept what the Bible says. Like Satan in the Garden of Eden they ask, 'Did God really say'?

They want to say that they are Christians and so they plant doubt in the mind of the believer, and they reinterpret the Bible in the light of their feelings and what our society says. For the Christian it has to be the other way round. We don't get to rewrite the Scriptures to suit us. On any issue. We read our society through the Scriptures, not the Scriptures through our society (or our feelings).

So in answer to your question, I would not tell you to go out and change your feelings. I would ask you simply, as I would ask myself or anyone – no matter their sexuality – which desire is going to rule your life? The desire to love and serve Jesus, or the desire to satisfy your own lusts?

CONSIDER: Do you think you can serve God and be single and celibate? Why do you think God gave us his instructions about marriage? Do you think your feelings can change? Remember that ultimately it is only God who is unchangeable. His Word cannot be changed.

RECOMMENDED FURTHER READING:
Why Does God Care Who I Sleep With? – Sam Alberry
Tales of an Unlikely Convert – Rosario Butterfield

PRAYER: Our Father, thank you for giving us freedom. Thank you that we are not robots, but that you want us willingly to love you. Thank you that you have not left us to ourselves, just to go our own way, but that you have given us your instructions. We confess O Lord, that we are not able to obey these without the aid of your Spirit. Cleanse us, renew us, forgive us, enable us to live for you. May our desires be yours, in Jesus Name, Amen.

51. EFFECTIVE PRAYER

QUESTION: How can I pray so that God answers my prayers?

BIBLE READING: Matthew 6:5-15

TEXT: 'This then is how you should pray: Our Father in heaven, hallowed be your name' (Matthew 6:9).

Prayer is difficult. Prayer is simple. Prayer is effective. Prayer is not a formula. Which is why your question needs to be rephrased or at least explained further. If you think that there is a formula for prayer: one Lord's prayer plus two hail Marys plus three from the Book of Common Prayer plus one week of 24/7 prayer, plus raising hands, kneeling or fasting, equals God's answer – you have completely misunderstood prayer.

Some people think that if God doesn't answer their prayer to pass their exam, get money or heal their cat then clearly God does not exist. They are right. The God who is at our beck and call, who is simply there like some kind of divine slot machine to give us what we ask does not exist. The God who has revealed himself to us in Scripture does. So, it is perhaps best to ask how he wants us to pray.

That is what the disciples did and Jesus in Matthew 6, answered by teaching them what we know as the Lord's Prayer. In *ASK* 39 and 40 we looked at this question of prayer and mentioned a great book on the subject Tim Keller's *Prayer – Experiencing Awe and Intimacy with God.* You will notice the title. It is not 'how to get God to answer your prayers', but rather how prayer enables us to know God better. There are very few books that have had such an impact upon me as this one. Not because it is the best book on prayer, but because it is like a compilation of all the best books I have read on prayer. Since I read it, I have changed the way I pray. Every day I use the Lord's Prayer – not as a magic formula – but rather as a pattern. Every day I use the book of prayers in the Bible – the Psalms. And every day I make sure that I read the Bible as the greatest aid to prayer.

Personally, I think the weakest area of my life is prayer. Not particularly in terms of answered prayer. I know that God always answers my prayers, when these prayers are requests, as he does yours. His answers can be split into three types – yes, no and wait.

Our prayers should not first of all be about our requests. They should be about God's glory. They should be praise before they are pleas. And when we ask, we need to ask in accordance with his will. When Jesus said, 'I will do whatever you ask in my name, so that the Father may be glorified in the Son.' (John 14:13) he was not giving a blank cheque to indulge our desires. He was telling us that when we pray in his name, in accordance with his will and seeking his glory, that will be given.

But how do we know what his will is? His revealed will is revealed in the Scriptures. Therefore, I can pray with confidence for God to save people, because that is what he has promised to do. It's what some older Christians called 'praying the promises'. But in order to pray them you need to know them.

So, what about the things that are not revealed in the Scriptures? For example, you may be praying about who you should marry. When Annabel was my girlfriend, I was thinking about whether I should propose. I got two very differing bits of advice. One older minister said to me, 'Do you love her? Can she cook? And does she know you are going to be a minister and is she supportive of that?'. If the answer was yes, then I should just get on with it! Another friend said that I should ask the Lord and he would reveal it to me through the Scriptures. He gave his own example – 'I prayed, and I read in the Song of Solomon – 'behold the rose of Sharon' so I married Sharon! I handed him a Bible and asked him to find Annabel in it for me!

We have to think about these things for ourselves. We use the principles of God's Word – but God's Word does not tell us exactly who to marry, or what job to do, or where we should live. But we can and should pray for guidance.

The book of James has some great principles for prayer for us. If we lack wisdom, we are to ask God in faith that he will grant it to us (1:5-8). We must humbly accept the Word planted in us and do it as well as hear it (1:22-25). When we ask God, we should do with right motives, not just seeking things for ourselves (4:1-3). We should submit to God, come near to him, humble ourselves before the Lord and he will come to us and lift us up (4:7-10). We pray when we are in trouble, we confess our sins to each other and then we will know what it is to be like Elijah. 'The prayer of a righteous man is powerful and effective'.

And there is the secret to effective prayer. To be right with God, seeking his heart and submitting to his will. Your will be done.

CONSIDER: Think about your own prayer life. Is it regular or spasmodic? Is it all about you? Or other people? Or God? Do you pray with other people? Why do you think it is that for most people, the church prayer meeting is the one that they are least likely to go to? Do you think it is okay to read written prayers? Do you have a prayer partner? If you are not a Christian, have you ever prayed to God to reveal himself to you, and to make you a Christian?

RECOMMENDED FURTHER READING:
Prayer – Experiencing Awe and Intimacy with God – Tim Keller
Booklet on Prayer – John Calvin
The Valley of Vision – A Collection of Puritan Prayers and Devotions.

PRAYER: I call to you Lord, come quickly to me; hear me when I call to you. May my prayer be set before you like incense; may the lifting of my hands be like the evening sacrifice' (Psalm 141:1-2).

52. KNOWING YOU ARE A CHRISTIAN

QUESTION: What is a Christian? How do you know you are Christian anyway?

BIBLE READING: 1 John 5:1-13

TEXT: 'Everyone who believes that Jesus is the Christ is born of God, and everyone who loves the father loves his child as well' (1 John 5:1).

Of all the questions in this book this is perhaps the most important one. We have been talking a lot about what Christians do or should do. And we have seen the importance of being a Christian. But what is a Christian, and how would you know that you are one? For those who are reading this I don't know most of you, I don't know your needs, or your personal circumstances, beliefs and desires, but I do know this – there is no bigger question for you than what do you think of Jesus? (Matthew 22:42).

We looked at this question in *ASK* (question 27), but just in case you don't have that book and because it is so important let me summarise what was said there. The word Christian is used in lots of different ways. It can just be a cultural term. Some people think that it means a 'good' person – you know the kind of people who say, 'that's not very Christian of you'. Did you know that the early Christians weren't even called Christians? They were known as disciples of Jesus, or followers of the Way. It wasn't until Barnabas and Saul had taught great numbers of people in the Syrian city of Antioch that they were first called Christians (Acts 11:26).

A Christian is basically a follower of Jesus Christ. If we go through 1 John 5:1-12 (indeed the whole of 1 John) we are told both what a Christian is and how we can know we are one. It's a matter of faith, love, obedience and life. This gives us the assurance that we belong to Christ. Let's deal with this in the form of questions.

Who do you have faith in? Who do you believe in? Everyone has faith. It may be in ourselves and our own judgement. It may be in others – in politicians, family, friends, or religious figures. But the Christian is someone who has faith in Christ. Not just belief about him, but trust in him. We trust his testimony. And so, we believe that he is the Messiah, the Son of God. That he gave himself for our sins. We commit our lives to him. He is our Saviour and our Lord. Belief about is not faith in. So, I ask again: What do you think of Christ? Do you have faith in him?

Who do you love? Being a Christian is not just an intellectual matter. It's not just signing up to a doctrinal statement. It's about who we love. What we love we give ourselves to. It's strange how many people claim to be Christians, yet they show no love to him.

By their actions they deny him. If I told you that I loved my wife, but I never spent any time with her, ignored her completely and never spoke about her, don't you think you would be entitled to question whether I really did love her? A Christian is someone who loves God, who loves his children, and who loves his Word.

Who do you obey? Love for God is not just a statement with our mouths, or a feeling within our hearts. It is expressed in obedience to him. John makes it clear; 'in fact this is love for God: to keep his commands' (v. 3). That is why some of the questions we have looked at in this book and in *ASK* are so important. We want to know what God says, so that we can obey him. This is not because we think that by obeying him we can save ourselves, but rather because we love him because he has saved us and we want to express our love to him, by obeying him.

Are you alive? Jesus promised that everyone who believed in him would have eternal life. He tells us to come to him that we may have life. God has given us eternal life and this life is in his Son. To have Christ, is to have life. Whoever has the Son of God has life, whoever does not have the Son of God does not have life.

How can you know? We can look at all these factors. We can examine ourselves to see whether we are in the faith. But most of all we can look to Christ. In my earlier Christian life sometimes, I wasn't sure if I was a Christian, so I simply prayed: Lord I'm not sure if I am a Christian, but if I am not, please make me one. I believed, and still believe, that he will never turn away anyone who comes to him. (John 6:37). That is what we call blessed assurance. It's an assurance that comes from the character, beauty and work of Christ - not from ourselves. 'If our hearts condemn us, we know that God is greater than our hearts, and he knows everything'

(1 John3: 20). Trust Jesus with everything. If you do, you are a Christian.

CONSIDER: You cannot believe in Jesus unless you know about Jesus. How will you get to know? How can you believe his promises unless you know them? Find out what they are by reading his Word.

RECOMMENDED FURTHER READING:
Magnificent Obsession – David Robertson (a book I wrote for those who want to find out more about Jesus – if you can't get or afford a copy – drop me a request at ask.david@newchurches. org.au and I will see what we can do!).

PRAYER:
Lord Jesus Christ, there are many things I do not understand, grant me your light; there are many things I fear, grant me your love; there are many sins I have committed, grant me your forgiveness; take my life, all that I am, all that I have, all that I dream; and create in me a new life, a new spirit, a renewed mind. baptise me with your Holy Spirit, create in me a clean heart, forgive my sin. Welcome me into your church, your family, your bride. From now on enable me to live as your child seeking your kingdom, serving your people, saving your world. And when my time is come, take me to be with you in the new heavens and the new earth; where suffering, sin and sorrow,shall be no more. For Jesus' sake. Amen.

AND FINALLY

EVERYONE who believes that Jesus is the Christ is born of God, and everyone who loves the father loves his child as well' (1 John 5:1)

Thanks for reading this far – or dipping in and out. If you have any questions then I suggest you discuss them with Christian friends, family or Church. Or feel free to drop me a message on the *ASK* website – www.ask.org.au

I am thankful for many people who have helped me with this book. Thanks to my colleagues in ENC (Sydney Anglicans), the staff at Christian Focus, the teenage boys at North Sydney Boys' School, the youth group at St Thomas's, the teenagers who again wrote from all over the world. I'm sorry if your question was not included. But don't despair – after *ASK* and *SEEK* – God willing will come *KNOCK*.

When you knock on a door – it's a sign both that you are there and that you want in. When the Bible speaks about Jesus knocking at the door of our heart, it is a sign that he is there, and he wants in. There are a lot of personal issues that people have about this. That's why the next book will be *KNOCK*. If you have any questions, then please feel free to write me and perhaps we will be able to include them – ask.david@newchurches.org.au

I am so grateful for the support of my wife Annabel – our team is still going after thirty-six years! – and the rest of my family. Since *ASK* we have two new grandchildren – Lewis and Elianna – this book is dedicated to them as they grow up in this confused world – and to my father – who left it last year and is now enjoying the heaven we spoke of in some of the questions. To God be the Glory.

David Robertson, Sydney

APPENDIX: RECOMMENDED BOOKS

1. *Apocalypse Never: Why Environmental Alarmism Hurts Us All* – Michael Shellenberger
   A Different Shade of Green – Gordon Wilson
2. *What does the Bible Teach about Transgenderism?* – Owen Strachan and Gavin Peacock
   Irreversible Damage – Abigail Shirer
3. *That Hideous Strength* – C.S. Lewis
   Black Mass – John Gray
4. *Where is God in a Coronavirus World?* – John Lennox
5. *The Marvellous Pigness of Pigs: Respecting and Caring for All God's Creation* – Joel Salatin
6. *Faultlines* – Voddie Baucham
   The Illustrated Westminster Shorter Catechism – published by Christian Focus
7. *The Land of the Book – Scottish Christianity in a Year of Quotes* – Christian Heritage
   John Knox – The Sharpened Sword – Catherine Mackenzie
   At the Roots of a Nation: The Story of Colegio San Andrés, a Christian School in Lima, Peru – John Macpherson
8. *Right to Choose – The Effects of Post Abortion Trauma* – Maureen Long
   Counter Culture – David Platt
9. *Church and State; Good Neighbours and Good Friends* – essay in *Crown Him Lord of All*
   What is the Relationship between Church and State? – R.C. Sproul
   Dietrich Bonhoeffer – A Spoke in the Wheel – Dayspring MacLeod
10. *Christians – The Urgent Case for Jesus in our World* – Greg Sheridan
11. *Live not by Lies* – Rod Dreher
    1984 – George Orwell
12. *Issues Facing Christians Today: 4th Edition* – John Stott
13. *The Hiding Place* – Corrie Ten Boom
14. *Do Hard Things: A Teenage Rebellion Against Low Expectations* – Alex and Brett Harris
15. *Dying to Kill* – Kieran Beville
    A Christian's Pocket Guide to Understanding Suicide and Euthanasia – D Eryl Davies
16. *Holding On to Hope: A Pathway through Suffering to the Heart of God* – Nancy Guthrie
17. *Genesis 1 -4 – In the Beginning* – Roger Fawcett
18. *Unbreakable – What the Son of God said About the Word of God* – Andrew Wilson
19. *Where to Start with Islam* – Samuel Green
    Engaging with Hindus – Robin Thomson
20. *Sinful Speech* – Sins of the Tongue – John Flavel
21. *Job, the Wisdom of the Cross* – Christopher Ash
    Paradise Lost – John Milton
22. *Baa Baa Doo Baa Baa: The Memory Verses* – Colin Buchanan
    My 1st Book of Memory Verses – Carine MacKenzie
23. *The New Testament Documents – Are They Reliable?* – F F Bruce
24. *Genesis* – Derek Kidner
    The Serpent and the Serpent Slayer – Andrew David Naselli
25. *Blessed* – Nancy Guthrie
26. *The Last Battle* – C.S. Lewis
27. *Do Muslims and Christians Worship the Same God?* – Andy Bannister
    Where to Start with Islam – Samuel Green
28. *Chosen by God* – R.C. Sproul

29. *Did the Devil Make me do it?* – Mike McKinley
    Satan Cast Out – Frederick S. Leahy
30. *What Happens When I Die?* – Marcus Nodder
    What Happens When We Die? – Chris Morphew
31. *Who Am I?* – Jerry Bridges
32. *The Momentous Event* – W.J. Grier
33. *Art and the Bible* – Francis A. Schaeffer
    Modern Art and the Death of a Culture – Hans Rookmaaker
34. *Come Let Us Sing* – Rob Smith
35. *Principles of Mathematics Book 1* – Katherine Loop
36. *Beautifully Distinct – Conversations with Friends on Faith, Life and Culture* – Ed Trillia
    Newbell (Good Book Company)
    The Four Loves – C.S. Lewis
37. *Knowing God* – J.I. Packer
38. *The Dawkins Letters* – David Robertson
39. *The Cross of Christ* – John Stott
    Forgive – Tim Keller
40. *The Good of God – Enjoying Father, Son and Holy Spirit* – Mike Reeves
41. *Fear Not – What the Bible has to say about Angels, Demons, the Occult and Satan* –
    Simon Van Bruchem.
    How Could a Loving God Send Anyone to Hell? – Benjamin M. Skaug
42. *What is Man?* A. Craig Troxel
    What Makes us Human? – Mark Meynell
43. *God's Good Design: What the Bible Really Says About Men and Women* – Claire Smith
    Men and Women in the Church – Kevin DeYoung
    God's Design for Women – Biblical Womanhood for Today – Sharon James
44. *Erasing Hell* – Francis Chan and Preston Sprinkle
    Christianity for Modern Pagans – Peter Kreeft
45. *Engaging with Atheists* – David Robertson
    Evangelism and the Sovereignty of God – J.I. Packer
    Making Faith Magnetic – Daniel Strange
46. *Jesus Ascended* – Gerrit Scott Dawson
    The Ascension: Humanity in the Presence of God – Tim Chester and Jonny Woodrow.
    The Ascension of Christ – Patrick Schreiner
47. *Nothing in my Hand I Bring* – Ray Galea
    A Christian's Pocket Guide to Papacy – Leonardo De Chirico
    Jesus of Nazareth – Pope Benedict XVI
48. *Evangelical Truth* – A personal plea for unity, integrity and faithfulness – John
    Stott
    Christianity and Liberalism – J. Gresham Machen
49. *Indwelling Sin – How Do I Kill Remaining Sin* – Geoff Thomas
    Gentle and Lowly – The Heart of Christ for Sufferers and Sinners – Dane Ortlund
50. *Why Does God Care Who I Sleep With?* Sam Alberry
    Tales of an Unlikely Convert – Rosario Butterfield
51. *Prayer – Experiencing Awe and Intimacy with God* – Tim Keller
    Booklet on Prayer – John Calvin
    The Valley of Vision – A Collection of Puritan Prayers and Devotions.
52. *Magnificent Obsession* – David Robertson

CHRISTIAN FOCUS PUBLICATIONS

Christian Focus Publications publishes books for adults and children under its four main imprints: Christian Focus, CF4K, Mentor and Christian Heritage. Our books reflect our conviction that God's Word is reliable and Jesus is the way to know him, and live for ever with him.

Our children's publication list covers pre-school to early teens. We also publish personal and family devotional titles, biographies and inspirational stories that children will love.

From pre-school board books to teenage apologetics, we have it covered!

Christian Focus Publications Ltd,

Geanies House, Fearn, Ross-shire,

IV20 1TW, Scotland,

United Kingdom.

www.christianfocus.com

CHRISTIAN FOCUS PUBLICATIONS

CF4•K
*Because you're never
too young to know Jesus*